How to Use Your Snap Revision Text Guide

This *Refugee Boy* Snap Revision Text Guide will help you get a top mark in your Edexcel English Literature exam. It is divided into two-page topics so that you can easily find help for the bits you find tricky. This book covers everything you will need to know for the exam:

Plot: what happens in the play?

Setting and Context: what periods, places, events and attitudes are relevant to understanding the play?

Characters: who are the main characters, how are they presented, and how do they change?

Themes: what ideas does the author explore in the play, and how are they shown?

The Exam: what kinds of question will come up in your exam, and how can you get top marks?

To help you get ready for your exam, each two-page topic includes the following:

Key Quotations to Learn

Short quotations to memorise that will allow you to analyse in the exam and boost your grade.

Summary

A recap of the most important points covered in the topic.

Sample Analysis

An example of the kind of analysis that the examiner will be looking for.

Quick Test

A quick-fire test to check you can remember the main points from the topic.

Exam Practice

A short writing task so you can practise applying what you've covered in the topic.

Glossary

A handy list of words you will find useful when revising *Refugee Boy* with easy-to-understand definitions.

AUTHOR:

STEVE EDDY

ebook

To access the ebook versi Snap Revision Text Guide,

collins.co.uk/ebooks

and follow the step-by-step instructions.

T0309414

Published by Collins
An imprint of HarperCollins*Publishers*
1 London Bridge Street
London SE1 9GF

HarperCollins*Publishers*
Macken House
39/40 Mayor Street Upper
Dublin 1
D01 C9W8
Ireland

© HarperCollins*Publishers* Limited 2022

ISBN 978-0-00-852031-1

First published 2022

10 9 8 7 6 5 4 3

British Library Cataloguing in Publication
Data.

A CIP record of this book is available from
the British Library.

Commissioning Editor: Claire Souza
Project managers: Fiona Watson and
Shelley Teasdale
Author: Steve Eddy
Copy editor: Fiona Watson
Proofreader: Charlotte Christensen
Reviewers: Rebecca White and
Djamila Boothman
Typesetting: Q2A Media
Cover designers: Kneath Associates and
Sarah Duxbury
Production: Karen Nulty

Printed in the United Kingdom

ACKNOWLEDGEMENTS
© Lemn Sissay and Benjamin Zephaniah,
2013, Refugee Boy, Methuen Drama, an
imprint of Bloomsbury Publishing Plc.

MIX
Paper | Supporting
responsible forestry
FSC
www.fsc.org   FSC™ C007454

This book contains FSC™ certified paper and other controlled
sources to ensure responsible forest management.

For more information visit: www.harpercollins.co.uk/green

Contents

Scenes 1–4

You must be able to: understand the situation Alem finds himself in at the start of the play.

How does the play begin?

Scene 1 presents a **symbolic dialogue** between Alem and his father, Mr Kelo, who identifies the North Star and tells Alem that in England the stars 'take it in turns to shine'.

How does Alem feel when he discovers his father has left him on his own?

Awaking in a London hotel room in Scene 2, Alem is alarmed to find his father gone and the door locked. Mr Hardwick, the hotel manager, lets himself in, attempting a joke about Alem making as much noise as an elephant.

Alem, disorientated, speaks at first in an Ethiopian language. Hardwick thinks Alem does not speak English. Alem is distressed and screams. He even thinks he must still be asleep. Hardwick tries to reassure him, but is himself nervous, moving towards Alem 'like he's a snared tiger'.

Hardwick leaves a letter from Mr Kelo on the floor for Alem. It is spoken to the audience by the characters of Alem and Mr Kelo, and reveals that Mr Kelo is leaving Alem in London for his own safety. Alem reacts with sadness, then anger.

What is Alem's first day in the children's home like?

Unlike the novel, the play shifts straight from the hotel room to a children's home. Alem meets Mustapha, who talks a lot, jumps rapidly from one idea to the next and is a poor listener.

Mustapha is much more interested in Alem's chips than in Alem's name. Alem seems to comment ironically on this when he says, '*Do you want those chips* is a strange name.' This playfully introduces the theme of identity.

There is a comic moment when Mustapha asks, 'Do you know who I am?' and Alem replies, 'No, that is why I am asking you.'

Alem does not want Mustapha to get into trouble over the chips, and Mustapha shows humanity in telling Alem to be careful in the home. Appropriately, the bully Sweeney arrives at this point and talks about 'thrashing' the others at table tennis later. Sweeney asserts himself as 'top dog' by insisting on calling Alem 'Ali', but saying he will hurt anyone who alters his own name.

How does Mustapha let Alem down?

In Scene 4, Alem and Mustapha are at the bus stop, with Mustapha demonstrating his obsession with cars. Mustapha is trying to educate Alem in the use of English slang when Sweeney turns up. Once again he asserts his status by playing with Mustapha's name and telling him that Ruth, a girl at school, is out of his 'league'. There is a veiled threat in Sweeney's words when he talks about Alem being lucky and getting pocket money. He seems to wilfully misunderstand Alem, accusing him of disrespecting his (Sweeney's) family. Mustapha tries to intervene but Sweeney launches into a racist diatribe against refugees, punches Alem, takes out a knife and forces him to say 'I am a Refugee Boy'. Mustapha seems to side with Sweeney, and leaves with him.

Key Quotations to Learn

Mr Kelo: In England the stars have to sleep. They take it in turns to shine. (Scene 1)

Mr Kelo: Remember to love your neighbours because peace is better than war … (Scene 2)

Sweeney: Your country don't want you and it don't want you because you're liars and thieves … (Scene 4)

Summary

- Alem is distressed to find himself alone in London.
- In the children's home, Alem meets talkative Mustapha, who tries to help him.
- Sweeney is a children's home resident who wants to be at the top of the pecking order.
- Sweeney accuses Alem of insulting his family. Mustapha tries to intervene.
- Sweeney makes a racist anti-refugee speech and threatens Alem. Mustapha leaves with Sweeney.

Questions

QUICK TEST
1. According to Mr Kelo, how do stars in England save energy?
2. Where does Scene 2 take place?
3. What is Mustapha obsessed with?
4. What does Mustapha try to teach Alem?
5. What does Sweeney force Alem to do?

EXAM PRACTICE
Write a paragraph explaining what difficulties Alem has experienced so far.

You must be able to: understand why Mr Kelo brings Alem to London and how Alem settles in with his **foster** family.

How do we learn what problems Alem's family faced in Ethiopia?

Scene 5 is set in Ethiopia. A young soldier breaks into the Kelo family's home and demands to know if Mr Kelo is Ethiopian or Eritrean. He hits Mrs Kelo, whom he calls an enemy 'whore' – she is Eritrean. He calls Alem a 'mongrel' because of his mixed parentage.

The scene is presented as if it is being played out in Mr Kelo's memory. He explains that this incident made the family flee to Eritrea.

The end of this scene presents Alem running away from the children's home. He defiantly insists that he is not running away but searching for his father.

Alem's **monologue** shows how young black males often experience the police. He says he will not speak to them.

How does Alem settle in?

Scene 6 jumps to the home of the Fitzgeralds, who are foster parents. Mrs Fitzgerald and her daughter Ruth try to help Mr Fitzgerald find his wallet. Alem shows his helpfulness by bringing in Mr Fitzgerald's coat: the wallet is in a pocket. Mr Fitzgerald declares that Alem is 'good luck'.

Ruth tells her parents how popular Alem is at school, but also seems to want them to take an interest in her. The family seems happy, but there are undercurrents of tension in their dialogue. Mr Fitzgerald complains that he has not been told that Alem will have to go to court. Mrs Fitzgerald stops Ruth from singing a song from the musical *Oliver*, and Mr Fitzgerald quietly intervenes, simply saying his wife's name.

There is also mention of Themba, another boy the Fitzgeralds fostered. Mrs Fitzgerald is sensitive about him being mentioned, and does not want Ruth to compare Alem with him.

The cheese knife going missing is an example of **foreshadowing**. It will be significant later.

How is Alem's relationship with his father shown?

Scene 7 does not advance the plot, but it shows the father–son relationship, and Alem getting used to England. Mr Kelo patiently passes on his knowledge. He repeats the playful idea from Scene 1 that the stars in England take it in turns to shine, but then explains that they cannot be seen clearly because of light pollution – unlike in Ethiopia.

The stars could symbolise human virtue, which is easier to see in contrast with evil. The North Star could symbolise the 'guiding light' of virtue leading Alem through his life.

How is the upcoming court hearing introduced?

Scene 8 follows up on the earlier mention of the court hearing. Alem has very negative expectations, having heard that court is where people are unjustly sent to prison. Mrs Fitzgerald reassures him.

The family warn Alem what to expect, even though it is 'just a formality'. Alem is confused about why he has to apply for permission to stay in England when he wants to go home.

The scene ends with Alem and Ruth alone together. She has heard him crying at night. She is hurt when he retaliates by saying he has heard her crying over Themba.

Key Quotations to Learn

Soldier: Leave Ethiopia or die! Your choice, Mr Kelo. (Scene 5)

Ruth [about Alem]: Everyone's like, pleased to see him now. (Scene 6)

Alem: It [court] is where they lock you into prison for being a traitor to your country even if you are not … (Scene 8)

Summary

- In Ethiopia, Mr Kelo is called a traitor for marrying an Eritrean woman.
- Alem runs away from the children's home and enters a foster family.
- Alem is settling in well at school and with the foster family.
- Mr Kelo teaches Alem about stars.
- Alem will have to get permission to remain in England.

Questions

QUICK TEST
1. What nationality is Mrs Kelo?
2. Why does Mr Fitzgerald say Alem is 'good luck'?
3. What is the name of the boy previously fostered by the Fitzgeralds?
4. Why is Alem confused about having to go to court?
5. What have Alem and Ruth heard each other doing at night?

EXAM PRACTICE
Write a paragraph explaining what seems to be going well for Alem so far.

Scenes 9–12

You must be able to: understand what leads up to the news of Mrs Kelo's death.

What happens when Alem first goes to court?

The Fitzgerald family act out the episode of Alem going to court. This is a dramatic **device** rather than a realistic scene. It avoids having to introduce new characters or actors.

In a long monologue, Alem tells the court (and the audience) who he is and where he comes from. He shows respect for his father when he says that his father can speak six languages. Alem can 'only' speak three.

The case is adjourned while Alem's lawyer gathers more information. Alem wishes the court Merry Christmas, because it is Christmas Day in Ethiopia.

How do Alem and Mustapha re-establish their friendship?

Alem and Mustapha find themselves at the same bus stop. At first they do not speak, but Mustapha breaks the silence. He apologises for not supporting Alem against Sweeney's bullying. Alem has discussed it with Ruth, who has pointed out that Mustapha was Sweeney's victim too.

Having forgiven Mustapha, Alem invites him back to the Fitzgeralds'. Mustapha is unable to go because he is on curfew for pouring paint over the roof of the children's home. He believes that rules are made to be broken.

Their playful banter shows they are friends again, and that Alem has picked up more English slang.

What leads up to the news of Mrs Kelo's death?

Scene 11 begins with the Fitzgeralds discussing Alem. Mr Fitzgerald is unhappy about Alem staying for longer and becoming increasingly part of the family. This is because he worries about his wife becoming attached to Alem, as she did to Themba, and then being hurt when Alem leaves.

The tensions in the family come more to the surface when Mr Fitzgerald announces that Alem will be with them for longer, and that he is now 'part of our family'.

Ruth, remembering Themba, complains to her mother that she is 'doing it all again' – becoming attached. She is also unhappy about losing five pounds – and perhaps wants her parents to focus some attention on her. Generously, Alem insists on giving her his own money.

Mr Fitzgerald gives Alem a letter, which Alem opens and reads to himself (but audibly to the audience). In it, Mr Kelo breaks the news of Mrs Kelo's murder. There is **dramatic irony** in the fact that at this point only Alem and the audience know that she is dead. The Fitzgeralds must be confused and alarmed when Alem becomes distressed and thinks his father is at the door. The audience will hear the banging (which reminds us – but not the Fitzgeralds – of the soldier in Scene 5).

What happens to the Kelo family in Eritrea?

What happens to the Kelo family in Eritrea echoes what happened to them in Ethiopia. A soldier accuses Mr Kelo of grovelling before Mengistu (the President of Ethiopia) then coming to Eritrea like a 'scavenger'. He forces Mr Kelo to dance at gunpoint. Confusingly, the soldier asks, 'What kind of woman are you?' and says, 'This woman is a traitor.' Since Mrs Kelo is not in the scene, he must be insulting Mr Kelo.

 ## Key Quotations to Learn

Alem: I would like to wish you all a Merry, Merry Christmas. (Scene 9)

Mustapha: Poured paint on the roof from the top window … (Scene 10)

Mr Fitzgerald [to his wife]: I can see what's happening. I just don't want you hurt. (Scene 11)

 ## Summary

- Alem's case is adjourned.
- Alem and Mustapha renew their friendship.
- Both Mr Fitzgerald and Ruth worry what will happen if Alem becomes part of the family.
- Mr Kelo's letter breaks the news of Mrs Kelo's murder to Alem.
- We see that the Kelo family were treated as traitors in Eritrea, just as in Ethiopia.

 ## Questions

QUICK TEST
1. How many languages can Mr Kelo speak?
2. Why has Mustapha been put on curfew?
3. Why are Mr Fitzgerald and Ruth worried about Mrs Fitzgerald?
4. What has Ruth lost?
5. Who calls Mr Kelo a 'scavenger'?

EXAM PRACTICE
Write a paragraph about the dramatic effect of Mr Kelo's letter arriving.

You must be able to: comment on how Alem is changing as he reacts to his mother's death.

How have the Fitzgeralds been affected by the death of Themba?

Ruth tells her mother that Alem has 'a time-bomb strapped on the inside of him', meaning that sooner or later he will explode. They argue about whether Ruth was consulted about fostering Alem.

The underlying issue emerges: the Fitzgeralds are still overcoming the trauma of Themba's death. Ruth says they need to talk about him, but Mrs Fitzgerald says she can't. Ruth misses him.

How do Ruth and Alem become closer?

In Scene 14, Ruth goes to see Alem in his room, where he has been grieving his mother. She explains why she is 'just a bit suspicious' of him. She refers to Themba: 'One I fell for. He died. He killed himself.' Despite her caution, she says Alem can trust her like a sister.

The mood changes when Alem sees snow falling for the first time. He is enchanted, but Ruth just sees it as a nuisance. Suddenly, Alem is hit by the knowledge of his mother's death. He hugs Ruth and 'sobs his heart out'.

How does Alem assert himself and avoid having his bike stolen?

Alem and Mustapha have a friendly conversation. Mustapha commiserates with Alem over his mother's death, but still comments on every passing car. Mustapha admits that he likes school, and Alem says that he likes it 'very much', listing its good points in a way that Mustapha sees as excessive: 'It may be good but it's not that good.'

The friends talk briefly about Themba, who was Mustapha's 'mate', about football, and even about Charles Dickens. Alem enjoys reading Dickens, but Mustapha just finds his novels difficult.

Mustapha hints that the reason for him being in the home has something to do with his father being driven away and never coming back – hence his car obsession.

Another boy, 'Hooded', tries to take Alem's bike. Unlike in Zephaniah's novel, in which Alem gives up his bike, here he responds to the boy's threat by taking out the Fitzgeralds' cheese knife and threatening to cut the boy's throat. In contrast with Scene 4, in which Alem gives in to Sweeney and says 'I am Refugee Boy', here he angrily orders the boy to say his real name. He frightens the boy by implying that he is as tough as his war-torn background.

In a surprising twist, Sweeney arrives and defends Alem, telling 'Hooded' to leave. However, he teases Alem about the cheese knife and advises him, 'You don't wanna get into knife fights.' Sweeney also reveals that his father used to beat him up.

Is there flirtation between Alem and Ruth?

Alem tells Ruth a version of the attempted bike theft story – in which he was confronted by more than one boy. He exaggerates what he told the boy, making up details of horrors in Africa. He does not mention Sweeney. Ruth is impressed, but then he admits to her that he is making it up, and she playfully goes to punch him. He jokes that she is 'trying to mug' him and the scene ends in a **cliffhanger** with a possibly flirtatious stand-off.

Key Quotations to Learn

Ruth: Can't you see there's like, a time-bomb strapped on the inside of him? (Scene 13)

Alem: I know where I'm going. I know where I'm from. (Scene 15)

Sweeney: You don't want to be like us, Alem. Messed with. Messed up. (Scene 15)

Summary

- Ruth and her mother argue about fostering another child after Themba.
- Ruth explains why she is cautious about foster children. Alem is distraught about his mother.
- Mustapha and Alem have a friendly chat. They both admit to liking school.
- A boy tries to take Alem's bike, but Alem threatens to cut his throat. Sweeney intervenes.
- Alem gives Ruth an exaggerated version of the attempted mugging.

Questions

QUICK TEST
1. What does Mrs Fitzgerald find hard to talk about?
2. What was Ruth's relationship with Themba?
3. What does Alem see for the first time in Scene 14?
4. What advice does Sweeney give Alem?
5. How does Alem alter the story of the attempted bike theft?

EXAM PRACTICE
Write a paragraph about how Alem develops in these scenes.

You must be able to: write about the tensions around Mr Kelo's return, the court's decision and the campaign to overturn it.

What happens when Mr Kelo arrives?

There is awkwardness when Mr Kelo comes to the Fitzgeralds' home. They were expecting him, but not so soon. The unease shows in little misunderstandings. For example, when he says, 'It's been quite a journey', the Fitzgeralds think he means from Eritrea, not Shepherd's Bush in London. When they ask him how he likes his tea, he thinks they are asking how he likes the situation.

Mr Kelo cannot understand why he cannot just take Alem away. The Fitzgeralds explain that there are 'procedures' to be followed now that Alem has been left in their care: Alem is a **ward of court**. Mr Fitzgerald even asks him for identification. Fortunately, Alem himself enters with Ruth at this point.

The Fitzgeralds give Mr Kelo thirty pounds, which he wants to spend taking them all for a meal. After more awkwardness, he agrees to talk to Alem in the Fitzgeralds' kitchen instead. He tells Alem he has claimed **asylum** for them both.

How are Mr Kelo and Alem refused asylum?

As in Scene 9, the Fitzgeralds act out what happens when the Kelos' asylum case is heard. They now take different roles.

Mr Fitzgerald, as the representative of the government, argues that there is no real war between Ethiopia and Eritrea. He claims it is just a series of border skirmishes, so 'the risk to the lives of the appellants is minimal' and they should go back and move further away from the border. Ruth, as their lawyer, argues that in fact there has been a 'massive escalation of the fighting'. She also points out that the Kelos were persecuted by both sides for being a mixed-race family. Finally, she reveals that Mrs Kelo has been 'hacked to death'. Shocked by this awful description, Alem screams, then faints.

In an **expressionistic** section, Mr Kelo yearns for his wife's return. When he says, 'Take it back, take it back and take *him* instead', he is presumably wishing that he could give his own life (not Alem's) in return for having his wife alive again.

Despite the **tragic** loss of Mrs Kelo, the Adjudicator (acted by Mrs Fitzgerald) refuses Mr Kelo and Alem asylum.

How is the anti-deportation campaign started?

Scene 19 jumps to Ruth and Mustapha planning a campaign to overturn the court's decision. Their energy and enthusiasm is evident. Ruth is project leader and Mustapha her assistant. Mustapha's affection for Alem is apparent, while Ruth demonstrates her respect: 'Alem, it's your story. You are heading the campaign. You're the refugee.'

Alem agrees and asserts himself, pointing out that the campaign slogan should be 'The Kelos Must Stay', not 'Free the Kelos', because they are not in prison.

Ruth and Mustapha plan a poster, leaflets, radio publicity, collecting money and a band. This is an example of shared community action.

Key Quotations to Learn

Mr Kelo: We must ask this great country of Dickens and Shakespeare to let us stay and make a home for ourselves here. (Scene 17)

Ruth [as the lawyer]: At this point there is no place for what is a mixed race family in this conflict. (Scene 18)

Alem: Damn right. I'm the refugee. I'm the boy. I'm the refugee boy. (Scene 19)

Summary

- Mr Kelo comes to the Fitzgeralds' home to fetch Alem. They say Alem cannot leave immediately.
- The Fitzgeralds give Mr Kelo some money. He wants to spend it on taking them out for a meal to thank them for looking after Alem, but they persuade him to talk to Alem in their kitchen.
- The court turns down the Kelos' asylum application on the grounds that they will be safe in Africa.
- Ruth and Mustapha organise a campaign to stop the deportation.

Questions

QUICK TEST
1. Why can't Mr Kelo take Alem away immediately?
2. Why does Alem scream and then faint?
3. Why are the Kelos refused asylum?
4. Who is project leader of the anti-deportation campaign?
5. What do Ruth and Mustapha plan for the campaign?

EXAM PRACTICE
Explain how the arguments of the two sides in the asylum court case differ.

You must be able to: write about the conflict between Alem and his father, and how the anti-deportation campaign is interwoven with the lead-up to Mr Kelo's murder.

How do Alem and his father fall out?

Mr Kelo is horrified when he hears about the campaign, insisting that they should wait for the appeal and 'be as peaceful as possible. Make no fuss.' Alem does not share his father's trust in the law. He also shows his new influences: 'Jah knows what will happen to us if we get sent back?' Mr Kelo objects to his son's new way of speaking, and his growing independence.

Alem stands up for his own views, accusing his father of betraying his mother, who 'was a fighter and would not stay quiet'. Mr Kelo angrily orders Alem out of 'his' house and even raises a hand to hit him.

A poetic section at the end of Scene 20 expresses Mr Kelo's grief over his wife, and Alem's disappointment in his father.

How does Mustapha begin the anti-deportation campaign?

The campaign gets underway on the street, and Mustapha addresses the crowd. He gives a short, simple speech in which he says that he is Alem's best friend and that the court, in the form of people unlike him and Alem, and with no knowledge of their world, will claim that the Kelos should be deported from Britain. He then makes way for Ruth.

How are scenes from the two settings inter-cut?

The playwright Sissay creates a quickening of the dramatic pace by shortening the scenes and switching rapidly between what is happening in the campaign and what is happening to Mr Kelo. In Scene 22, Mr Kelo encounters Tewdros, a man from the East African Solidarity Trust. Mr Kelo tells the man that he is no longer a member of EAST and tells him firmly to go away.

Scene 23 returns to the campaign. Ruth is giving a speech in which she declares, 'Alem and his father deserve the right to live without fear.' She says that the march they have organised is 'an example of youth power'. Then she calls on Alem to take the stand.

How does it become apparent what is happening to Mr Kelo?

Scene 24 is somewhat mysterious. A man, presumably Tewdros from Scene 22, seems at first to sympathise with Mr Kelo, as if they are on the same side against the authorities who 'make us jump through hoops … strip us of our, of our, dignity'. A **stage direction** describes Mr Kelo 'detecting something', but it is not clear what. It could be a hint of danger in the man's manner, or perhaps the knife in his pocket. There is also menace in the man's enigmatic 'Great danger, Mr Kelo,' even though he appears to be sympathetic.

Another stage direction indicates that Mr Kelo 'understands what is happening', though the audience may not at this point. He must be realising that the man intends to kill him.

Key Quotations to Learn

Mr Kelo: No campaign. No more politics. This has nothing to do with us. (Scene 20)

Mustapha: Never really known who I was. Spent a life in different homes. (Scene 21)

Ruth: We are all brothers and sisters. (Scene 23)

Summary

- Mr Kelo objects to the campaign. He and Alem argue, and Mr Kelo almost hits Alem.
- Mustapha addresses the crowd, saying he likes to think of himself as Alem's best friend.
- Ruth addresses the crowd and expresses solidarity with Alem.
- Mr Kelo is approached by a man from EAST who seems to represent a threat to him.

Questions

QUICK TEST
1. How does Mr Kelo think he and Alem should respond to the court's decision?
2. What does Alem accuse his father of?
3. How does the playwright quicken the dramatic pace?
4. Who is the first to address the campaign crowd?
5. Of which organisation is the man who approaches Mr Kelo a member?

EXAM PRACTICE
Summarise what Mr Kelo thinks of Alem's words and behaviour at this point.

You must be able to: analyse how the play reaches its final **climax**.

How does Alem address the crowd?

Alem reveals himself to be an effective speaker. He says he can't understand why he is in England. This is partly because he can't understand why Ethiopia and Eritrea are fighting over 'a border that is mainly dust and rocks'.

Alem lightens the tone for a moment by joking about how cold England is. He then lists the stages that Ethiopia and Eritrea will have to go through before they can achieve peace: talking, negotiating, drawing up a treaty, agreeing on it and signing it. Alem shows that, like his father, he is interested in achieving more than just his own security. He promotes 'a culture of peace'.

How does Mr Kelo die?

Mr Kelo's conversation with the mysteriously menacing Tewdros continues in Scene 26. The man says that Alem is 'gaining too much attention'. Perhaps he wants the war to continue and objects to Alem promoting peace. Mr Kelo repeats what he told Alem – that he should not get involved in politics. Interestingly, in Zephaniah's novel, Mr Kelo is persuaded to support the campaign, but in the play he remains opposed to it.

Tewdros seems particularly sinister when he hushes Mr Kelo before stabbing him.

How does Alem champion world peace in his second speech?

Alem voices even wider ambitions. Appropriately, he reveals that his name means 'World', and that he wants world peace, with no refugees, and people travelling the world freely.

He brings the speech back to the personal level when he says how hard the loss of his mother has been. Then, in another moment of dramatic irony, he invites his father to come up. He assumes that his father is in the crowd.

There is a sense of the **narrative** drawing to a close with the radio report of Mr Kelo's murder in Scene 28. The news report has the effect of 'zooming out' cinematically from the close-up of the murder in Scene 26. It says that 'the killing may have been politically motivated'.

The report mentions Alem having 'earned the respect of many young people in the east of London' and says he is now 'devastated'. This credits Alem in a way that provides a fitting conclusion to the play, valuing his contribution to the cause of peace. It also avoids ending the play with a scene of distress in close-up.

How does the play end?

The final scene is almost the same as Scene 1, which focuses on the closeness between Alem and his father. The difference is that Alem now speaks the lines about the North Star that were previously his father's. This suggests that he has learned from his father and can now survive on his own.

The play ends, however, with another mysterious repeated line, in which Alem pleads with his father to let him go with him. In Scene 7, this line is about Alem wanting to join his father on his walk, and his father refusing. Now, at the end of the play, the line suggests that Alem wants to follow in his father's footsteps as a peacemaker.

Key Quotations to Learn

Alem: We must become that new generation of peacemakers. (Scene 25)

Mr Kelo: He should not be involved in politics! (Scene 26)

Alem: I would like my father to come up here and introduce himself to you. (Scene 27)

Summary

- Alem makes a speech about the Ethiopian–Eritrean conflict, which to him is senseless.
- A mysterious man, Tewdros, stabs Mr Kelo.
- Alem speaks out in support of world peace at the West Indian Centre.
- The radio news reports the murder of Mr Kelo.
- The play ends as it began, with a conversation about the stars.

Questions

QUICK TEST
1. What, according to Alem, does the border between Ethiopia and Eritrea mostly consist of?
2. What complaint does Mr Kelo's murderer make about Alem?
3. What final wish does Alem express in his big speech?
4. What does the radio report say Alem has earned?
5. What key difference is there between the play's opening and closing scenes?

EXAM PRACTICE
Write a paragraph about what impression of Alem these final scenes give.

Narrative Structure

You must be able to: analyse the play's narrative development.

What kind of plot does the play have?

The play is about a **protagonist**, Alem, growing up, or 'coming of age'. In the case of a novel, this kind of story can be called a **bildungsroman**. This form of story can be traced back to **myths** in which a hero loses his father, or both parents, and has to find his own identity. Like the typical hero, Alem has helpers – Mustapha and Ruth. A modern version of this type of hero is Harry Potter.

The play's narrative challenges Alem in ways which all contribute to his growing up.

What challenges does Alem face?

Alem has already experienced difficulties before coming to England. His family has been persecuted by soldiers and he has been called 'a dirty poison, a mongrel' (Scene 5) because of his mixed parentage. The play reveals this past in two **flashback** scenes.

The play presents Alem's challenges, then shows how he deals with them. In England, his first challenge is finding himself alone in a London hotel. Then in the children's home he experiences racist bullying from Sweeney, who forces him to say he is 'a Refugee Boy' – a label he later embraces as part of his identity (Scene 19).

After Alem escapes the children's home (Scene 5), his next challenge is to fit into the Fitzgerald household. This is easier, but it is here that he learns about his mother's murder, followed by the court's refusal of the Kelos' asylum application.

News of his mother's murder helps to push Alem into the next stage of his growing up – the stage of angry rebellion he is in when 'Hooded' attempts to take his bike and he fiercely defends himself. Interestingly, it is the bullying Sweeney who intervenes and advises Alem against going down the path of violence that he has taken himself. This moment, when Alem could turn towards violence or peace, could be seen as the play's **crisis point**.

How does Alem develop?

In terms of narrative structure, Alem's development emerges from his challenges. He becomes a peacemaker, but rejects his father's passive, respectful attitude towards the law. His standing up to the English legal system, and in the process standing up to his father, is an important part of his growing up. Yet he does not reject or disrespect his father, as we see when he says he would like him to introduce himself to the campaign supporters (Scene 27).

Alem becomes a champion of peace, but one who is willing to fight for it, and for his own rights, through political protest.

How is the narrative presented?

Parts of the narrative are told in flashback, taking us back in time to the persecution of the family in Africa. Scene 5 is set in Ethiopia, though it is told partly as Mr Kelo's recollection. Scene 12 tells the story of the family's similar treatment in Eritrea from the viewpoint of Alem's memory.

The narrative becomes **non-linear** in a different sense towards the end as the scenes become shorter and the playwright switches rapidly between characters and settings, speeding up the pace as the play approaches its climax. Scenes showing the protest are **juxtaposed** with short scenes leading up to Mr Kelo's murder.

The final scene is almost identical to the first. The main change is that Alem understands the lines about the North Star, perhaps showing that he has learned, and is taking over from his father.

Key Quotations to Learn

Alem: I am a Refugee Boy. (Scene 4)

Alem: If you mess with me one more time, I'll cut you up. (Scene 15)

Alem: What we really need is a culture of peace. (Scene 25)

Summary

- The play charts Alem's growing up.
- Alem grows up through facing challenges.
- Alem rebels against his father's passivity but still respects and loves him.
- Some scenes are told in flashback.
- Short scenes quicken the pace as the play approaches a climax.

Questions

QUICK TEST
1. What is a bildungsroman?
2. How does being left on his own help Alem to grow up?
3. Who are Alem's main helpers?
4. Why might the attempted bike theft be seen as the play's crisis point?
5. What is the dramatic effect of the short scenes near the end?

EXAM PRACTICE
Draw a storyline showing what you consider to be the play's five or six key moments.

A Play Adapted from a Novel

You must be able to: write about the relationship between the play and the novel it is based on.

How did Benjamin Zephaniah come to write the novel?

Zephaniah was born in Birmingham in 1958, of Afro-Caribbean immigrant parents. He is dyslexic and has stated that he was illiterate when he left school aged 13. Even later, he was not a keen reader, preferring books to be short. Before writing novels, he became known as a performance poet. When he wrote *Refugee Boy*, he wanted to write a novel that his teenage self might have read – although the novel is much longer than the play.

What were Zephaniah's influences?

Zephaniah cites as his influences Martin Luther King, Malcolm X, Michael X, Angela Davis and Marcus Garvey, who were all involved in the politics of racial equality. He was also influenced by people he met as a young man while serving a prison sentence for burglary. This experience probably influenced his depiction of the British court system that Alem and his father face.

Zephaniah has visited refugee camps worldwide. He says in the novel's introduction that he wrote it 'because I realised that every day I was meeting refugees, and each one of them has a unique, and usually terrifying story to tell.' He speaks of the suffering and danger driving asylum-seekers.

How did Lemn Sissay come to write the stage version?

Zephaniah and Sissay have been friends since the 1980s. When a theatre suggested turning the novel into a play, Zephaniah wanted an unknown playwright to tackle it. Sissay was already well-known, but he persuaded the novelist that he was the right person because the story was so close to his own. Sissay was born in Wigan but his mother was Ethiopian, his father Eritrean. His unmarried mother's social worker placed him with foster parents when he was born; when he was 12, his foster parents returned him to **social services** and he then grew up in a children's home.

How is the play different from the novel?

First, the novel is 285 pages long, not 53. It tells the story **chronologically**, whereas the play includes flashbacks to Alem's African past, and cuts to new scenes with no intervening narrative. The novel begins in Ethiopia and Eritrea. It then shows Alem and his father coming through British customs, with a tense moment when it looks as if they might be detained. The play opens with a short scene establishing the father–son relationship, then cuts to Alem alone in the hotel.

The novel describes settings but the play does not use stage directions to do this. The novel describes the children's home at length; the play reveals just enough to show why

Alem hates it. A major difference is that in the novel Alem passively accepts his bike being stolen, whereas in the play he angrily asserts himself and threatens to cut the boy's throat. In the play, Sweeney arrives and takes Alem's side, but not in the novel.

The symbolic, poetic scenes in which Alem and his father discuss the stars are not in the novel. Nor is the poetic section after Mr Kelo almost hits Alem, nor the scene in which Sweeney rescues him.

The play is a stripped-down version of the novel which presents the key events and character relationships. There is less attempt to present the narrative realistically. For example, in the play, the Fitzgeralds represent people in the court scenes; the novel narrates them more conventionally.

Key Quotations to Learn

Mr Kelo: In England the stars have to sleep. (Scene 1)

Sweeney: Love your work. Rebel with a cheese knife. (Scene 15)

Mr Kelo: The room swoons, spins, and sways. All things permanent give way. (Scene 20)

Summary

- Zephaniah, son of immigrants, wrote the novel; Sissay, of Ethiopian and Eritrean parentage, wrote the play.
- Zephaniah has experience of courtrooms and refugee camps.
- The novel is a more joined-up **chronological** narrative than the play.
- In the play, Alem angrily defends himself when a youth wants his bike.
- The play conveys key ideas and events in a dramatic way.

Questions

QUICK TEST
1. Where was Zephaniah born?
2. How did Sissay's background echo the novel?
3. In which version do the Kelos go through customs?
4. How does a cheese knife feature in the play?
5. How are the lawyers and judge in the court scenes represented in the play?

EXAM PRACTICE
Write a paragraph about how Zephaniah's and Sissay's experiences relate to the play and the novel it is based on.

The Settings

You must be able to: write about what types of event take place in the different settings.

What is Alem's introduction to England?

Scenes in this play are defined by what happens in them. For example, the opening scene has no clear setting, though it is probably outdoors and in England. Scene 2 is in a London hotel. The long stage direction shows Alem waking in the room and becoming increasingly distressed because his father is missing, and because the door is locked.

Alem speaks in Amharic, which of course the hotel manager cannot understand. The scene therefore establishes England as a place of confusion and distress for Alem.

What is the children's home like?

The children's home is funded and supervised by social services – a department of local government. It gives food, shelter and some degree of security to young people who cannot be with their parents. As Mustapha puts it, some are there 'for trials, some for family reasons'.

Our first impression of the home is through Mustapha's complaint about getting too few chips at mealtimes. This shows it is run on a tight budget. It is also a place where residents have to cope with each other. Alem quickly finds out that bullying happens here. He meets Sweeney, who renames him 'Ali' to show his authority, and who, in the next scene, on the street, invents an excuse to punch him and threaten him with a knife.

What is the Fitzgeralds' home like?

It is characteristic of the representative nature of the dramatic narrative that the play does not show Alem's introduction by social workers to the Fitzgeralds, instead going straight into a scene in which Mr Fitzgerald has lost his wallet (Scene 6). His wife and daughter try to help him, which tells the audience that this is the type of family whose members help each other. When Alem quietly produces Mr Fitzgerald's coat, with his wallet in its pocket, this shows that he already fits in well.

The Fitzgerald home is a safe haven for Alem. Mr Fitzgerald worries that his wife will become too attached to Alem and then be hurt when he leaves. Apart from that, Alem is made very welcome, even by the teenage Ruth, although she too is cautious because of her past experience of foster children.

The Fitzgerald home, however, is also a place where things are hinted at but left unsaid. In particular, the parents are reluctant to talk about Themba, an immigrant boy they fostered who took his own life.

How does the playwright present Alem's African background?

Two flashback scenes (5 and 12) are inserted into the narrative in which we see the Kelo family persecuted first in Ethiopia and then in Eritrea. The scenes are similar, showing that the family are rejected and in danger wherever they go. They echo the first two chapters of the novel.

As the scenes are presented like memories, there is no attempt in the stage directions to describe the two family homes.

How is the courtroom shown?

Unlike the novel, the play makes no attempt to create an impression of the courtroom as a physical place. Rather, the key players are represented by the Fitzgerald family members, so all the emphasis is on the arguments put forward and the outcomes.

Key Quotations to Learn

Mustapha: There's like loads of people from all over the world in the home ... (Scene 4)

Eritrean soldier: Dirty dog traitors. (Scene 12)

Mrs Fitzgerald: I can't talk about Themba. (Scene 13)

Summary

- The play does not use stage directions to describe settings.
- Alem hates the children's home and feels unsafe there.
- The Fitzgeralds' home is a safe haven for Alem.
- The safety of the Fitzgerald home is contrasted with the danger of Ethiopia and Eritrea.
- There are undercurrents of tension in the Fitzgerald home.

Questions

QUICK TEST
1. What establishes England as a confusing and threatening place for Alem?
2. What does Mustapha complain about?
3. In what setting is Alem punched and threatened?
4. What two settings appear in flashback?
5. How far do stage directions describe the courtroom?

EXAM PRACTICE
Using one of the 'Key Quotations to Learn', write one or two paragraphs about a setting and why it is important in the play.

The Ethiopian–Eritrean Conflict

You must be able to: explain how the conflict leads to the Kelos being persecuted.

What is the basis of the conflict?

Both countries are in the 'Horn of Africa' – north-east Africa. Their dispute goes back a long way. Ethiopia is much larger, its population being more than thirty times that of Eritrea. However, crucially, it is landlocked. Possession of Eritrea would give it access to the sea.

Ethiopia has had a national identity for centuries, but Eritrea was a collection of kingdoms unified as an Italian colony in 1889. During World War Two, Eritrea was taken over by the British. In 1952, the United Nations declared it an independent country, but with political links to Ethiopia – a compromise between Ethiopian rule and complete independence.

Nearly ten years later, Ethiopia invaded Eritrea. Eritrea fought a war of independence against Ethiopia from 1961 to 1991. Tens of thousands died. Badme, on the border, Alem's hometown, was hotly disputed. In a 1993 referendum, almost all Eritreans voted for independence, but border conflicts continued, erupting into full-scale war in 1998. In 2000, both countries signed a treaty, but local conflict continues.

How are the Kelos affected?

Mr Kelo is Ethiopian, his wife Eritrean. Scenes 5 and 12 show them treated as traitors in both countries; Alem is referred to as a 'mongrel' – like a half-breed dog. It was Mrs Kelo's idea to found the East African Solidarity Trust (**acronym** EAST), to promote cooperation and peace between the countries.

The family try to live peacefully, first in Ethiopia, then in Eritrea. Continued persecution leads the parents to decide to try to move to England for Alem's sake.

How does the play's action depict the conflict?

Soldiers break into the family home and threaten them with death, first in Ethiopia (Scene 5), then Eritrea (Scene 12). The conflict leads to the murder of Mrs Kelo. This devastates Alem, who briefly seems to embrace violence himself, before becoming a champion of peace by the end of the play.

Sadly, the conflict pursues Mr Kelo to London. It is not revealed who murdered Mrs Kelo, but Mr Kelo is killed by a man called Tewdros who claims to be from EAST. He objects to Alem speaking out for peace, and may want the war to continue.

What views of the conflict are depicted in the courtroom?

The lawyer acting for Mr Kelo and Alem says that they will be in real danger if they return to Africa. During the second court scene, we hear the brutal evidence that Mrs Kelo has been 'hacked to death'. According to the lawyer (spoken by Ruth), there has been 'a massive escalation of the fighting'.

The lawyer for the Secretary of State, resisting the asylum application, claims that there is just 'a border pursuit' or even 'a skirmish' between the countries.

Key Quotations to Learn

Soldier: You choose your homeland like a hyena picking and choosing where he steals his next meal from. (Scene 12)

Mr Fitzgerald [representing the Secretary of State]: Most of the people in Ethiopia and Eritrea have not seen any fighting whatsoever. (Scene 18)

Alem: In my homeland they are fighting over a border, a border that is mainly dust and rocks. (Scene 25)

Summary

- Ethiopia and Eritrea are in north-east Africa. Ethiopia claimed a right to rule Eritrea, which wanted independence.
- Eritrea fought for independence for thirty years. There was full-scale war from 1998 to 2000. Relations remain tense.
- Mr Kelo is Ethiopian, Mrs Kelo Eritrean; the family are persecuted in both countries. This is shown in scenes in which soldiers threaten them and insult Alem.
- Mrs Kelo is murdered in Africa, Mr Kelo in London by a man who claims to be from EAST.
- The Secretary of State claims that Mr Kelo and Alem can live safely in Africa; their lawyer claims otherwise.

Questions

QUICK TEST
1. Which has a bigger population, Ethiopia or Eritrea?
2. What town does Alem come from?
3. Why is Alem referred to as a 'mongrel'?
4. What does the acronym EAST stand for?
5. What does the lawyer for the Secretary of State claim?

EXAM PRACTICE
Using one or more of the 'Key Quotations to Learn', write one or two paragraphs explaining how the family is persecuted in Africa and threatened with deportation in England.

Becoming a Refugee and Seeking Asylum

You must be able to: explain in what sense Alem and Mr Kelo are refugees and what they face when seeking asylum.

What is a refugee?

The 1951 United Nations Refugee Convention defines a refugee as someone who, 'owing to a well-founded fear of being persecuted for reasons of race, religion, nationality, membership of a particular social group, or political opinion', is outside their country and cannot be protected by it.

The plot of the play hinges on whether Mr Kelo's fear of persecution both in Ethiopia and Eritrea is 'well-founded' – justified by the facts. His lawyer says it is; the lawyer for the Secretary of State (in effect the UK Government) says it is not.

In the novel, a charity, the Refugee Council, mentioned by Mr Kelo in Scene 20, gets Alem into the children's home.

What is asylum?

Asylum means a place of safety, a refuge. An asylum-seeker is someone who applies to a country's government for 'refugee status' so that they can remain in that country. Mr Kelo cannot apply to the UK Government for asylum from abroad: he has to be in the UK to apply. Someone in his position can either try to resettle in another nearby country like Sudan – where the security situation has remained volatile for a number of years – or seek to apply for asylum in a country considered to be safer.

Thousands of people in this situation (or similar) cross the Channel in small boats, often supplied at a considerable cost by 'people smugglers'. Mr Kelo enters the UK claiming to be on holiday, and then claims asylum. However, his first aim is to ensure Alem's safety by leaving him in the UK. He hopes to take Alem back to Africa when 'the fighting stops and our persecution is over'.

Like many other asylum-seekers, Mr Kelo is placed in poor, shoddy accommodation and is not allowed to work. In 2022, asylum-seekers were given less than £40 a week to live on by the Government.

How do Alem and Mr Kelo disagree about responding to the UK justice system?

Mr Kelo is a law-abiding man who respects and trusts the UK's legal system. He has become involved in politics in Ethiopia and Eritrea, but only as a peacemaker. When he and Alem are denied asylum (Scene 18), he says they should wait patiently for the appeal: 'We should be as peaceful as possible.' He even says they should just go home if told to by the judge.

Alem, on the other hand, is more proactive: he wants to take action to achieve their goals, rather than passively waiting and obeying. He is also more pragmatic – aware of the real situation. He does not share Mr Kelo's faith in the law: 'The judge doesn't know anything about Ethiopia or Eritrea.' He wants to put pressure on the UK Government by protesting.

Key Quotations to Learn

Ruth [as lawyer]: This is a family that is in fear for their lives. (Scene 18)

Mrs Fitzgerald [as Adjudicator]: … I cannot make a judgement based on emotions. (Scene 18)

Mr Kelo: Make no fuss. We cannot afford to draw attention to ourselves. (Scene 20)

Summary

- A refugee is someone who leaves their country because they have a justified fear of persecution.
- The Kelos' asylum application hinges on whether their fears of persecution are justified.
- An asylum-seeker is someone who wants to be granted refugee status and to live and work in a country.
- Mr Kelo trusts the UK legal system and thinks he and Alem should wait for their appeal and go home if they are told to.
- Alem thinks they should put pressure on the Government so they will be allowed to stay.

Questions

QUICK TEST
1. What must be 'well-founded' in order for someone to qualify as a refugee?
2. What is Mr Kelo's long-term aim when he brings Alem to England?
3. Why does Mr Kelo not just apply for asylum from his home in Eritrea?
4. What does Mr Kelo think he and Alem should do if their appeal fails?
5. How does Alem criticise the judge?

EXAM PRACTICE
Using one or more of the 'Key Quotations to Learn', write one or two paragraphs explaining how asylum laws are central to the play's story.

Children's Homes and Fostering

You must be able to: explain why Alem is sent to a children's home and then a foster family, and what his experience is of both.

What is a children's home?

A children's home is a large house where young people who cannot be with their own families live together. This could be temporary or long-term. The home provides shelter, food and opportunities for recreation. Children are looked after by professional staff.

Children might be placed in a home because social services judges that their parents are unable to look after them. Their parents could be mentally, emotionally or physically unwell, and a decision may be reached that a period of separation is in the best interests of the children. A **minor** cannot legally be left to fend for themselves.

Sweeney gives an insight into the background of some children in children's homes. His own experience is that 'Family messes you up'. Mustapha gives another insight. He is always hoping to see his father again. He is speaking **ironically** when he says, 'yeah, all our dads'll be here soon, man'. This suggests that many of the children would like to see their fathers again, but will be disappointed.

What is a foster home?

Young people can be placed with a foster family, like the Fitzgeralds, as an alternative to a children's home. Sometimes, foster parents go on to adopt a child they foster. The foster parents do not get paid a wage for fostering a child, but they do get paid expenses.

Social services employs staff to find suitable foster homes, depending on the needs of the child and the situation of the parents. Foster parents know from the start that the arrangement may be temporary, as it is intended to be with Alem.

Lemn Sissay is certainly qualified to write about both fostering and children's homes. He was fostered from infancy to the age of 12, when his foster parents put him into a children's home – the first of four he lived in up to the age of 17.

What is Alem's experience of both places?

In Zephaniah's novel, there is more description of the children's home and Alem's running away. Even in the play, it is clear that Alem is not happy there. He runs away (Scene 5) just after Sweeney attacks him (Scene 4). He does make friends with Mustapha, but his only other experience there is negative.

Alem's experience of the Fitzgeralds, on the other hand, is positive. They are friendly and supportive. Their teenage daughter Ruth is also kind to Alem, even though she has reason to be wary of foster children. She does fall out with Alem when he says he hears her crying over Themba (Scene 8), but later she tells him he can trust her like a sister (Scene 14).

The Fitzgeralds support Alem through his asylum application. Dramatically, their involvement may be hinted at by them playing the roles of the lawyers in court – although this is also a device to avoid having more actors on stage.

Key Quotations to Learn

Mustapha: We get chores. We got to wash up after twenty people. (Scene 4)

Mrs Fitzgerald: Home where? Where do you want to send him? (Scene 11)

Mr Fitzgerald: He's a fine boy. You must be proud. We've got used to having him around. (Scene 17)

Summary

- A children's home provides shelter to young people who cannot be with their families.
- Some children in children's homes come from dysfunctional families.
- A foster family offers relative security and support to a young person as an alternative to a children's home.
- Alem is bullied in the children's home and dislikes it enough to run away.
- He is happy with the Fitzgeralds, despite the personal losses he endures.

Questions

QUICK TEST
1. Who gives a negative view of family life based on his own?
2. What organisation puts Alem into the children's home?
3. Who does Alem make friends with in the children's home?
4. Why does Alem fall out with Ruth?
5. What dramatic device implies that the Fitzgeralds are involved in Alem's asylum application?

EXAM PRACTICE
Write a paragraph explaining why Alem is better off with the Fitzgeralds than in the children's home.

You must be able to: understand how the play presents the character of Alem.

How does Alem display an enquiring mind?

Scene 1 shows Alem asking his father about the stars. The discussion continues in Scene 7 and shows that Alem is a fast learner. He also shows this when Mustapha teaches him slang in Scene 4. Alem is always keen to learn. He enjoys school, saying it is 'great', and that he likes the challenge of reading Dickens. He says 'it's difficult but that's how I learn' (Scene 15).

How is Alem's likeable nature shown?

We first see Alem's generous spirit when he lies (unnecessarily) about his chips in order to protect Mustapha. In his first scene in the Fitzgerald home, he helps Mr Fitzgerald to find his wallet, and in Scene 11 he insists on giving Ruth his pocket money to replace money she has lost.

He also makes himself popular at school. Ruth says how well he has settled in: 'They love him. Everyone's like, pleased to see him now' (Scene 6).

What is Alem's relationship with his parents?

Alem respects and trusts his father, never questioning his wisdom in bringing him to England and leaving him on his own there. The opening scene establishes this respect. He is bullied by Sweeney in Scene 4 when he stands up for his parents, and Sweeney chooses to take this as a criticism of his own.

Alem is devasted when he hears that his mother has been murdered (Scene 11). When he eventually rebels against his father's passive acceptance of English justice, he calls on his mother's memory to support him: 'We are here because Mother was a fighter and would not stay quiet' (Scene 20).

How does Alem assert himself?

Much of Alem's growing up involves him asserting himself as an individual with rights – including a right to live in England. The play emphasises the importance of his name. He resists Sweeney trying to rename him, insisting that his name is Alem. However, to avoid being hurt he says, 'I am a Refugee Boy' (Scene 4). Sweeney wants to label him, denying his real individuality.

Alem changes after his mother dies. When a youth demands his bike (Scene 15), Alem defends himself. He repeatedly tells the youth to call him by his name, and threatens him with a cheese knife. This knife goes missing in Scene 6, suggesting that Alem was already thinking at this point that he might have to defend himself.

Alem asserts himself more effectively when he disagrees with his father over the planned protest march. By this point, Alem has embraced the name 'Refugee Boy' as part of his identity.

Key Quotations to Learn

Alem: I'd said I did not want my chips. I offered them to him. (Scene 3)

Alem: My family don't act like sinners. My father is a good man. And so is my mother. (Scene 4)

Alem: What's my name? My full name? Say my name. (Scene 15)

Summary

- Alem has an enquiring mind and is a fast learner.
- He is generous and helpful, and quickly becomes popular.
- He loves and respects his parents and is devastated by their loss.
- He asserts his rights as an individual, embracing his background as part of his identity.

Sample Analysis

Alem is ready to make the most of what England has to offer. He tells the Fitzgeralds that school is 'great', and lists his subjects (Scene 6). He also tells Mustapha that it is 'full of possibilities' (Scene 15). This shows that he is keen to learn. He even enjoys reading Dickens' *Great Expectations*, which Mustapha finds very difficult. Dickens' novel is also about a boy who has lost both parents and has to find his own identity, so Zephaniah's choice of it may foreshadow Alem's situation.

Questions

QUICK TEST
1. What does Alem lie about to protect Mustapha?
2. Who does Alem defend from Sweeney's criticism?
3. Why is *Great Expectations* an appropriate novel for Alem to like?
4. What does Alem use to threaten the youth?
5. Over what issue does Alem rebel against his father?

EXAM PRACTICE
Using one or more of the 'Key Quotations to Learn', explain how Alem develops as a character.

You must be able to: understand how the play presents the character of Mr Kelo.

Why does Mr Kelo leave Alem on his own in London?

We can see from Scene 1 that Mr Kelo is a patient and loving father – so loving in fact that he decides to take Alem to London for his own safety, telling him that it is for a holiday (Scene 7). In reality, he and his wife have decided that Alem should stay in England to be safe. In his letter to Alem, he writes: 'We value your life more than anything' (Scene 2).

Mr Kelo must anticipate Alem's alarm at finding himself alone in a London hotel room, but he must have decided that it will be easier for Alem this way.

What does Mr Kelo expect when he returns to England?

Mr Kelo intends to leave Alem in London only until the family can live safely in Africa. This plan changes after Mrs Kelo's murder. Mr Kelo then decides that he and Alem must try to make a life for themselves in England.

Mr Kelo returns to England intending to apply for asylum, which will enable him to work and Alem to be educated. He expects Alem to continue obeying him as he did in Eritrea and Ethiopia. He disapproves of Alem using the informal 'Dad', and is angry when Alem challenges him over the asylum appeal – so much so that, uncharacteristically, he raises his hand to hit him (Scene 20).

What is Mr Kelo's attitude to the British legal system?

Mr Kelo thinks England is a great country, and he respects its legal system. He believes, even after their asylum application has been refused, that the judge 'will weigh up the evidence and make his decision on the basis of fact and truth' (Scene 20). He is prepared to return to Africa if the judge orders it.

How and why does Mr Kelo die?

The reason for Mr Kelo's murder is unclear. He tells Alem that he has been to the London offices of EAST, that the organisation is now 'full of spies', and that there are 'murderers and criminals' being granted asylum. Mr Kelo himself is a peacemaker, both in Africa and England.

In Scene 26 there is a hint that Mr Kelo is murdered because 'Alem is gaining too much attention'. Although a stage direction in Scene 24 says that Mr Kelo 'understands what is happening', he seems powerless to stop it. He seems to be a helpless victim – even a naïve one.

Key Quotations to Learn

Alem: This is the best holiday I have ever, ever, ever ... (Scene 7)

Mr Kelo: We must ask this great country of Dickens and Shakespeare to let us stay and make a home for ourselves here. (Scene 17)

Mr Kelo: We gave everything to the cause of peace. Everything. And now we lose everything? (Scene 24)

Summary

- Mr Kelo means well when he tricks Alem into coming to England for a holiday and then leaves him there.
- Mr Kelo only intends Alem to stay in England until it is safe in Africa.
- After his wife's death, Mr Kelo decides to seek asylum for himself and Alem in England.
- Mr Kelo trusts the British legal system.
- Mr Kelo is shocked when Alem dares to challenge his views.

Sample Analysis

Sissay presents Mr Kelo as a well-intentioned, peace-loving man. His letter reveals that he is leaving Alem in London for his own safety. He knows that life in Ethiopia or Eritrea would endanger the family because they are hated by both sides. He is used to Alem being an obedient, respectful son, and is not prepared for him questioning authority in an independent way that is more typical of teenagers in England. He almost hits Alem, despite his non-violent principles, which shows how shocked he is.

Questions

QUICK TEST
1. What reason does Mr Kelo give Alem for their going to London?
2. What event makes Mr Kelo return to London?
3. How does Alem anger Mr Kelo?
4. Which two writers does Mr Kelo associate with England?
5. What problem does Mr Kelo identify in EAST?

EXAM PRACTICE
Using one or more of the 'Key Quotations to Learn', write one or two paragraphs explaining how Mr Kelo's plans go wrong.

You must be able to: understand how Mustapha is presented as Alem's friend.

What is Mustapha like?

Mustapha is the first person Alem meets in the children's home. He initially comes across as someone who is talkative, not always a good listener – he is at first only interested in Alem's chips – and who questions rules. His first words are 'Pisses me off, man', which shows his frustration with the lack of chips in his meal, and with the children's home generally. Later, in Scene 10, he rebelliously pours paint on its roof, and is punished by being put on curfew.

He tries to stay on the right side of Sweeney, conceding that Sweeney would 'thrash' him at table tennis, and giving Sweeney his chips, although moments earlier he wanted Alem's. When Alem questions this, Mustapha shuts him up for his own good. However, he does maintain some self-respect with Sweeney, telling him to 'Fa fa fakoff', though he is immediately conciliatory: 'Joke. Joking.'

He tends to jump from one idea to another. In particular, he will interrupt anything he or anyone else is saying to comment on a passing car. A stage direction says that he 'loves cars'. He claims his father is a mechanic.

How does Mustapha let Alem down?

Mustapha is good-natured and helpful, giving Alem advice on surviving in the children's home and teaching him slang (Scene 4). However, he finds himself torn between fear of Sweeney and his desire to help Alem. In Scene 4, he helps Sweeney to 'get' Alem's name – 'Like A Lem' – and when Sweeney seems to think that Alem is 'talkin' bad' about his family, he tries to calm him down: 'Sweeney, you know he wasn't.'

Realising that Alem cannot defend himself against Sweeney, Mustapha encourages him to give in and say, 'I am a Refugee Boy'. When he lets Sweeney punch Alem and threaten him with a knife, Mustapha could be seen as cowardly or just realistic. However, when he walks away with Sweeney, this might seem like more of a betrayal.

How does Mustapha become Alem's best friend?

After Alem has moved in with the Fitzgeralds, he meets Mustapha at the bus stop. Mustapha shows his generosity of spirit by saying he's pleased to see Alem in a better situation ('that's great'), even though he remains in the children's home himself. He also shows maturity by apologising for letting Alem down. Alem forgives him by saying that Sweeney was also bullying Mustapha, and by inviting him back to the Fitzgeralds' with him. From this point on, the pair become firm friends.

Later, Mustapha becomes a key helper for Alem, joining with Ruth to organise the anti-deportation campaign. He shows that, though not a great public speaker, he is a loyal and supportive friend.

Key Quotations to Learn

Mustapha: Keep your head down and everything will be all right. (Scene 4)

Mustapha: I'm sorry, man. I didn't mean for that to happen. (Scene 10)

Mustapha: They set up rules for breaking. (Scene 10)

Summary

- Mustapha has a lively mind and a rebellious nature.
- He shows his basic good nature by trying to help Alem survive in the children's home and teaching him slang.
- Mustapha is bullied by Sweeney and allows him to bully Alem.
- Mustapha has the courage to apologise for letting Alem down.
- He becomes Alem's best friend and helps organise the protest.

Sample Analysis

In the context of a children's home in which teenagers are cooped up together with too few staff, bullying is often common – as the playwright would know from his own experience. It could, therefore, be argued that Mustapha is just showing an instinct for survival when he fails to intervene when Sweeney attacks Alem. His later remorse is shown when he apologises.

Questions

QUICK TEST
1. Who is the first person Alem meets in the children's home?
2. What job does Mustapha say his father does?
3. What does Mustapha tell Alem to say to avoid a beating?
4. How is Mustapha punished for pouring paint over the children's home roof?
5. How does Mustapha help Alem later in the play?

EXAM PRACTICE
Plan an essay arguing for or against the view that Mustapha always behaves like a true friend to Alem.

You must be able to: write about Sweeney being an **ambiguous** character.

How does Sweeney behave like a bully?

Sweeney could be called the **antagonist** who challenges the protagonist, Alem. When he first appears, in Scene 3, he seems relatively harmless. He asks Mustapha if he wants to play table tennis, and says he'd 'thrash' him. The first real hint that he insists on getting his own way is when he gives Alem the nickname Ali, and then ignores Alem when he repeats his real name.

Sweeney's bullying becomes more apparent when he demands Mustapha's chips, clearly not expecting a refusal. Then he makes his need for respect obvious by telling Alem, 'If anyone calls me anything else but Sweeney I break their fingers and I slice them.'

Sweeney seems highly volatile. He is either very sensitive about his family, or else he wilfully misunderstands Alem in Scene 4 when he accuses him of calling his family 'sinners'. He goes into a racist rant about refugees, then grabs Alem, punches him and threatens him with a knife, forcing him to call himself 'Refugee Boy'.

How do we know about Sweeney's background?

Sweeney is presumably voicing his own negative experience when he says 'Family messes you up.' He must see his own family as hypocritical and dishonest, taking him to church and then acting 'like sinners for the rest of the week'. We can deduce from this that he is probably in a children's home because of difficult circumstances in his family home.

Sweeney is more explicit about his family in Scene 15 when he tells Alem that he is going deaf because his father used to beat him up. He blames this for his being 'in the shit' now.

How does Sweeney behave unexpectedly?

Having attacked Alem without provocation in Scene 4, Sweeney surprisingly comes to Alem's rescue in Scene 15, using his personal status to get rid of the youth who wants Alem's bike. This is when he reveals his past family life. He even displays a sense of humour, teasing Alem about his cheese knife, comparing him to the cheese-loving Wallace in the *Wallace and Gromit* films.

The moment when Sweeney strokes Alem's face and tells him not to spoil it in knife fights is open to interpretation. This could be a slightly sinister assertion of his power: he can get away with invading Alem's physical space. It could be an innocent gesture showing that even a bully can have a kinder side, and that he respects Alem being different from him. However, given that boys in the children's home could see physical displays of affection as unmanly, it might also be interpreted as suggesting that Sweeney is sexually attracted to Alem.

Key Quotations to Learn

Sweeney: Saw you checking out Ruth today, Musty. Get off. She's out of your league man. (Scene 4)

Sweeney: Used to beat me. Used to try and rearrange my face for me. (Scene 15)

Sweeney: You don't wanna get into knife fights. Cut up that good smooth skin of yours. (Scene 15)

Summary

- Sweeney is a bully. He needs to be regarded as dominant.
- He is volatile, suddenly subjecting Alem to racist abuse and attacking him for no reason.
- He also comes to Alem's rescue.
- He has a sense of humour.
- He used to get beaten up by his father. This is probably why he is in the home.

Sample Analysis

Lemn Sissay portrays Sweeney as a three-dimensional character, giving him depth by adding the scene in which he defends Alem from a would-be bike thief. This does not happen in Zephaniah's novel. Sissay may be drawing on his own teenage experience of children's homes when he implies that Sweeney is a bully because he was bullied by his father: 'Used to beat me.' This suggests that Sweeney now takes out his anger on those weaker than him, as his father did.

Questions

QUICK TEST
1. What game does Sweeney want Mustapha to play?
2. What does Sweeney give Alem?
3. What does Sweeney like to be called?
4. How does Sweeney come to Alem's rescue?
5. What is the implied reason for Sweeney being a bully?

EXAM PRACTICE
Using one or more of the 'Key Quotations to Learn', write a paragraph explaining in what ways Sweeney is an ambiguous character.

You must be able to: write about Mrs Fitzgerald's importance to Alem and her family.

Who is Mrs Fitzgerald?

The Fitzgeralds are experienced foster parents with whom Alem is placed by a social worker after he runs away from the children's home. Mrs Fitzgerald (Siobhan) is firm, efficient but caring, and generally works well with her husband in their fostering role.

The first impression Sissay gives of Mrs Fitzgerald is of a helpful woman who is better organised than her husband. She tries to help when he loses his wallet.

Her efficiency is shown when she tactfully deals with Mr Kelo when he thinks he can just take Alem away. She tells him that there are 'procedures' to follow (Scene 17). She also notices small details, like the missing cheese knife that Alem has taken for self-protection (Scene 6).

What does Mrs Fitzgerald find difficult to talk about?

Mrs Fitzgerald is a sensitive woman who is slightly touchy at times, as shown when, for no obvious reason, she stops Ruth from singing a song from the musical *Oliver*. She seems stressed: 'That's enough, Ruth. That's enough, I've heard enough' (Scene 6). It emerges that the Fitzgeralds have fostered other young people, including Themba, the most recent. It may be that Ruth's singing somehow reminds Mrs Fitzgerald of him.

Mrs Fitzgerald resists any talk about Themba, as she finds it too upsetting. Ruth thinks the family should talk about him taking his own life, but Mrs Fitzgerald thinks the family should bottle this up: 'If we all just said anything then where would we be?'

How does Mrs Fitzgerald show her kindness?

Mrs Fitzgerald helps Alem to prepare for his court appearance: 'There'll be lots of strangers asking you questions. Just answer them truthfully' (Scene 8). She is also reassuringly optimistic when she tells him what to expect: 'What will happen is they'll be giving you permission to stay in this country.'

When Mr Fitzgerald complains about Alem staying for longer than 'a couple of months', Mrs Fitzgerald rhetorically demands, 'Where do you want to send him?'

How do we know Mrs Fitzgerald is stressed?

The fact that Mrs Fitzgerald cannot talk about Themba in itself suggests that she is stressed, but there are other clues too. She seems overworked, exasperatedly telling Ruth, 'I wish you would bring your washing down when I ask for it.' A moment later, Ruth implies that her mother takes on too much – 'fixing everyone else and everyone else's problems.' This leads Ruth to insist that they need to 'talk about Themba', provoking Mrs Fitzgerald to snap at her: 'I can't. I can't, okay?'

At another point, Mrs Fitzgerald comments that she needs a holiday (Scene 11), but not in her native Ireland.

Key Quotations to Learn

Mrs Fitzgerald [to Ruth]: One day you'll have to do your own washing and then you might, you might understand. (Scene 13)

Ruth [to her mother]: You're all about fixing the world and fixing everyone else … (Scene 13)

Mrs Fitzgerald [about Themba]: I can't think about him every day. Every God-forsaken day. (Scene 13)

Summary

- The Fitzgeralds are experienced foster parents. They foster Alem.
- Mr Fitzgerald does not want Alem to stay indefinitely; Mrs Fitzgerald puts Alem's welfare first.
- Mrs Fitzgerald cannot face talking about Themba, who took his own life.
- Mrs Fitzgerald is kind-hearted but firm.
- She feels the strain of the situation.

Sample Analysis

Mrs Fitzgerald is a firm but kind-hearted woman. As foster parents, she and her husband are paid expenses for Alem's care, but her main concern is his welfare. She asks her husband, 'Where do you want to send him?', meaning that he has nowhere else to go. This care for Alem is despite the fact that she is still suffering from the stress of their previous foster child taking his own life while in their care.

Questions

QUICK TEST
1. What does Mrs Fitzgerald notice is missing?
2. What does she wish Ruth would do when asked?
3. How does Mrs Fitzgerald advise Alem to answer questions in court?
4. What makes Mrs Fitzgerald snap at Ruth?
5. Where does Mrs Fitzgerald not want to go on holiday?

EXAM PRACTICE
Explain what stresses the character of Mrs Fitzgerald is under and how these are shown.

You must be able to: understand Mr Fitzgerald and his relationship with his wife.

How does Mr Fitzgerald work well with his wife?

The Fitzgeralds are both committed to fostering as a way to help young people, as Mrs Fitzgerald reminds her husband: 'you said it was "all well and good if we can help someone else then we should"' (Scene 11).

We also see how they support each other in Scene 8, when they tell Alem what to expect in court:

> Mrs Fitzgerald: And there'll be other people there who you won't know. He won't, will he?

> Mr Fitzgerald: No, he won't know them. And they'll be taking notes.

This shows that they are working towards the same goals.

How does Mr Fitzgerald show his care and concern?

Mr Fitzgerald wants to make Alem feel at home, as is suggested when he says, 'You'll be right at home here, boy' (Scene 6). He is helpful to Alem, too, when he works with his wife to prepare Alem for court, even though he doesn't like being in court himself: 'I don't like it there' (Scene 8).

Perhaps this dislike is the reason his wife has not told him about the court appearance. When she mentions it at dinner, he sensitively allows Ruth and Alem to speak before gently raising his objection: 'Court. Nobody told me about court' (Scene 6). He raises it again later in the scene. Although he and his wife usually work well together, in this respect he feels he has not been kept informed.

Although he cares about Alem's welfare, Mr Fitzgerald cares more about his wife, and worries that she will become attached to Alem and be hurt when he leaves. He tells her: 'I just don't want you hurt' (Scene 11). He shows his love for her in the same speech when he compares it to the stars.

How is Mr Fitzgerald presented as sensitive and conciliatory?

Mr Fitzgerald seems to act as a buffer between his wife and daughter. He does this very gently in Scene 6 when Mrs Fitzgerald tells Ruth to stop singing the song 'Oliver'. He simply speaks his wife's name, Siobhan, to make her aware that she is speaking harshly.

He shows tact in Scene 13 when he walks in, unseen, on a difficult conversation between the two. After listening to his wife complaining that she cannot talk about Themba, he goes and hugs her. To give them a moment alone together, he tells Ruth, 'Go and see if Alem's alright, love.' This avoids making it seem as if he is getting rid of her.

Key Quotations to Learn

Mr Fitzgerald [referring to Alem]: He's got to go home. (Scene 11)

Mr Fitzgerald [to Alem]: You are part of our family. (Scene 11)

Mr Fitzgerald [to Mr Kelo]: It'll be sad to see him go. (Scene 17)

Summary

- Mr Fitzgerald is a compassionate man and a committed foster parent.
- He and his wife are for the most part a good team.
- He dislikes being in court, and thinks his wife should have warned him about it.
- He worries about his wife being hurt when Alem leaves.
- He is sensitive and tactful towards his family, Alem and Mr Kelo.

Sample Analysis

Sissay, perhaps drawing on his own experience as a foster child, shows that the Fitzgeralds make a good team as foster parents, for example supporting each other in preparing Alem for his court appearance, which is necessary for him to be allowed to remain in England. He clearly loves his wife, telling her to count the stars and multiply them '… and you won't get close to how much I love you.' He says this to comfort her, and to explain why he doesn't want to risk her being hurt.

Questions

QUICK TEST
1. What has Mr Fitzgerald lost when he first appears on stage?
2. Why is he worried about Alem staying?
3. What does he feel about court?
4. How does he put his love for his wife into words?
5. How does he get Ruth to leave the room?

EXAM PRACTICE
Using one or more of the 'Key Quotations to Learn', write one or two paragraphs explaining the different aspects of Mr Fitzgerald's attitude towards Alem.

You must be able to: comment on Ruth's role in the family.

Who is Ruth?

Ruth is the Fitzgeralds' daughter. She is in the same year at school as Alem and they are both studying Dickens (Scene 6). Mustapha also sees her at school and finds her attractive: 'Man, she is hot' (Scene 4). She is a lively, outspoken girl who stands up for herself.

How does Ruth get on with her parents?

Ruth gets on well with her father, getting playfully cross with him, and teasing him about 'going senile' (Scene 6). He is kind to her. For example, when she enthusiastically tells the family about Alem ('He settled in much better than Themba'), he comments, 'That's great, Ruth.'

It is Mr Fitzgerald who encourages Ruth to sing 'Oliver' and who intervenes when his wife makes her stop. This is the first indication of tension between mother and daughter. The source is obviously Themba, the family's previous foster child. Ruth fell in love with him, as she later confides to Alem, then he took his own life.

Ruth feels she doesn't get enough attention from her parents because their focus is on the problems of their foster children – first Themba, now Alem. When she says, in Scene 6, 'So what did I do at school today?' it may be because her parents haven't asked. She also seems to resent the attention being on Alem in Scene 11 when she is worried about her lost money: 'That's all I was thinking about. About how to tell you and then this is all you want to talk about.' She thinks her mother doesn't make time for her: 'It's always later, isn't it?'

What is Ruth's relationship with Alem?

Despite feeling that her parents are preoccupied with him, Ruth definitely likes Alem. We see this when she gushingly tells her parents about him. At first, she says everyone's 'pleased to see him now', but when she says that he is 'funny too', this is her own opinion.

Their relationship falters when she asks him, 'Did you take my fiver?', and she initially refuses to accept his money. However, it is cemented after Alem hears of his mother's death. She explains why she is 'a bit suspicious' of foster children, and says he can trust her like a sister. She encourages him to put his hand out of the window to feel the snow, and in moments he is hugging her and sobbing over his mother.

They have another intimate moment when he tries to impress her with his account of the attempt to take his bike (Scene 16). When he admits his exaggeration, she playfully tries to thump him. The scene ends in an arguably flirtatious stand-off.

What is Ruth's role in the anti-deportation campaign?

Ruth announces herself as the campaign's project-leader, but she insists that Alem is heading it. She comes up with a slogan, has ideas for publicity, and movingly addresses the crowd (Scene 23).

Key Quotations to Learn

Ruth [to her mother]: You don't ask my opinion. Not unless you know what I'll say. (Scene 13)

Ruth [on previous foster children]: One I fell for. He died. He killed himself. (Scene 14)

Ruth [to Alem]: I wish I could take all those memories away for you. (Scene 16)

Summary

- Ruth is lively, outspoken and attractive.
- She sometimes resents her parents' fostering.
- She likes Alem and says he can trust her like a sister.
- She may also be romantically attracted to him.
- She is the project-leader of the anti-deportation campaign.

Sample Analysis

Ruth favours getting difficult feelings out in the open. Showing emotional maturity, she tells her mother, 'We need to talk about what we've been through' (Scene 13), and Mrs Fitzgerald says she can't. The playwright uses this basic difference in character between the two to create dramatic tension. It could be compared with the tension between Alem and his father over the campaign.

Questions

QUICK TEST
1. Who finds Ruth attractive at school?
2. What song does Ruth start to sing?
3. Who does Ruth suggest is going 'senile'?
4. What happened to the foster child Ruth 'fell for'?
5. What is Ruth's role in the campaign?

EXAM PRACTICE
Using one or more of the 'Key Quotations to Learn', write one or two paragraphs explaining why Ruth's relationship with Alem is not straightforward.

You must be able to: comment on the dramatic roles played by other characters.

What introduction to London does Mr Hardwick give Alem?

Mr Hardwick runs the hotel to which Mr Kelo has taken Alem. He doesn't want other guests disturbed by Alem, and jokes about there being an elephant in the bathroom, then asks Alem where his father is. He speaks slowly, hoping Alem will understand, and tries to reassure him: 'I'm not going to hurt you. I've a son myself. Just like you.' There is arguably a hint of racist ambivalence when he corrects himself: 'Not like you. But you know.'

In Zephaniah's novel, the first English person Alem encounters is a customs officer, but in the play it is Mr Hardwick. To him, Alem is a problem, as he is later for social services and the legal system.

How do the soldiers feature in the play?

The novel begins with two almost identical passages, the first set in Ethiopia, the second in Eritrea, in which soldiers kick down the Kelo family's door, threaten them at gunpoint, then tell them to leave the country 'or die'. Scenes 5 and 12 in the play serve the same purpose – to show that the family are unwelcome and in danger in both countries.

There are differences between the scenes. The stage direction for Scene 5 says 'We are in Ethiopia', whereas Scene 12 is identified as being in Alem's memory. In Scene 5, Mr Kelo recognises the soldier as a local boy: 'I know your parents.' This shows how neighbours can turn against each other in a conflict. Despite knowing Mr Kelo, the soldier's condemnation of the family is vicious, and he hits Mrs Kelo with his gun.

Another aspect of conflict is that being in the army means the soldier has shoes and a uniform and is 'well fed'. This shows that some people benefit from a war and want it to continue.

The Eritrean soldier wants revenge for casualties. The fact that he makes Mr Kelo dance at gunpoint, then laughs at him, shows that he enjoys his power and the excuse to wield it.

Who is Tewdros?

Tewdros is the sinister and enigmatic man in Scenes 22, 24 and 26. He says he is from EAST, which Mr Kelo has left. He may be one of the 'spies' that Mr Kelo says have infiltrated the organisation (Scene 20). In Scene 24, the man appears to sympathise with Mr Kelo ('We understand, Mr Kelo'), but when he says, 'What happened to your wife is sad. So sad', it sounds insincere. Mr Kelo, according to the stage direction, 'understands what is happening'.

The man seems even more sinister in Scene 26 when he hushes Mr Kelo before murdering him.

Key Quotations to Learn

Mr Hardwick: I'll call the people and we'll get this sorted. (Scene 2)

Ethiopian soldier: Now I have shoes. (Scene 5)

Eritrean soldier: Dance when I tell you to dance. (Scene 12)

Summary

- The hotel manager, Mr Hardwick, finds Alem and tries to calm him down.
- Both African scenes show soldiers making violent threats to the Kelo family.
- These scenes show that soldiers may enjoy the benefits of war, and may look for scapegoats.
- The sinister Tewdros murders Mr Kelo.

Sample Analysis

The scenes in Ethiopia and Eritrea vividly show how endangered the Kelos are in either country, justifying Alem's refugee status. However, the soldiers in each scene show different aspects of war. The Ethiopian soldier was Mr Kelo's neighbour, which shows how neighbours can turn against each other in war. The Eritrean soldier wants revenge: 'An eye for an eye. It's very simple.' This quotes the Bible's Old Testament, flagging up that in a war over borders there will be reprisals. It is as if he blames Mr Kelo personally: 'You know how many have died while you were in Ethiopia?'

Questions

QUICK TEST
1. Why does Mr Hardwick suggest that there is an elephant in the hotel room?
2. In which country does Mr Kelo recognise a soldier as a neighbour?
3. In what way does the Ethiopian soldier say he is better off in the army?
4. What does the Eritrean soldier blame Mr Kelo for?
5. Of what organisation is Tewdros a member?

EXAM PRACTICE
Write one or two paragraphs explaining the dramatic importance of the two scenes with soldiers.

Home and Belonging

You must be able to: understand how the play depicts the importance of home and belonging.

Where is Alem's original home?

As Alem tells the court in Scene 9, he was born in Badme, a town claimed by both Ethiopia and Eritrea. His family moved to Asmara in Eritrea, then to Harar in Ethiopia. So, by the time he reaches England, aged fourteen, he has already experienced several moves.

As we see in Scenes 5 and 12, soldiers threaten the family in both countries.

How at home is Alem in the children's home?

The play does not reveal much about the children's home – less than the novel. For example, we see little of the staff. We do see Alem making friends with Mustapha, and being racially abused and physically attacked by Sweeney. Not surprisingly, Alem does not feel secure, or 'at home', there.

How far does the Fitzgeralds' house become home for Alem?

Mr and Mrs Fitzgerald try to make Alem feel at home, even though they think his stay will be temporary. It is significant that they are both Irish and have made a home for themselves in London.

Alem gets on well with the family, including Ruth. However, he tells the court in Scene 9, 'I don't want to stay here. My father is coming.'

How is belonging portrayed?

The Ethiopian and Eritrean soldiers believe that the Kelos do not belong in either country. Mr Kelo identifies himself as African, as he tells the soldiers. Alem does not at first feel he belongs in England, but this changes as he makes friends, whom he refers to in his campaign speech in Scene 27. He also mentions that his name means 'World', which perhaps Zephaniah intended to show that he is a global citizen.

Sweeney recognises that Alem does not belong in the world of street violence (Scene 15).

How is language shown to be important to belonging?

Alem is proud that his father speaks six languages. Speaking a language is seen as part of belonging. Mr Hardwick does not expect Alem to understand English well, partly because, in his confusion, Alem reverts to Amharic, one of the main languages used in Ethiopia. Mr Kelo makes Alem speak English; he wants him to belong.

However, the play shows that there is more subtlety to a national language. Hence Mustapha is shown teaching Alem colloquial young people's English in the children's home

– for example, 'bad' meaning 'good'. By Scene 10, Alem knows enough 'street' language to have a playful exchange of insults with him, showing he is becoming **assimilated** into London youth culture. His father disapproves of the way he now speaks.

Key Quotations to Learn

Sweeney [to Alem]: You're in a home 'cause you are a useless piece of shit, Refugee Boy. (Scene 4)

Mr Fitzgerald: You'll be right at home here, boy. (Scene 6)

Mr Kelo [to the soldier]: I am African, like you. (Scene 12)

Summary

- Alem was born in Badme, near the Ethiopian–Eritrean border.
- Soldiers in both countries threaten the family.
- Alem does not feel 'at home' in the children's home.
- Alem feels more at home with the Fitzgeralds.
- Language is an important aspect of belonging.

Sample Analysis

Mr Kelo feels that he belongs in Africa, rather than just Ethiopia or Eritrea. When he gives up on the prospect of peace, and decides to apply for asylum in England, he tells Alem that he wants them to be able to 'stay and make a home for ourselves here' (Scene 17). This introduces the idea that it is possible to 'make a home' in a new place. Mr Kelo bravely persists, even though social services place him in a hostel that is 'not five star exactly' (Scene 17), reflecting the typical experience of asylum seekers.

Questions

QUICK TEST
1. In what city and country was Alem's second home?
2. What language other than English does Alem speak in the play?
3. What sort of language does Mustapha start to teach Alem?
4. What does 'Alem' mean in English?
5. How does Alem show that he is beginning to blend in with London youth culture?

EXAM PRACTICE
Plan an essay arguing for or against the statement that 'belonging' is the most important theme in the play.

Conflict

You must be able to: understand how the play explores the theme of conflict.

How is conflict at the root of the play?

The play's **inciting incident** is Mr Kelo leaving Alem in a London hotel room and returning to Africa – a drastic course of action for a loving father. However, he is driven to do this by the conflict between Ethiopia and Eritrea, and the persecution of the Kelos in both countries.

The play makes the threat to the family clear in the flashback scenes, Scenes 5 and 12, in which soldiers give them an ultimatum: leave or die.

How does Alem experience continued conflict in London?

Alem experiences conflict in the children's home and therefore runs away. His monologue at the end of Scene 6 reveals how he is questioned by the police, as if he has run away from home, and as if he might be a drug user. The playwright seems to be commenting on how young black males in London are likely to be treated by the police.

Alem is racially abused, punched and threatened at knifepoint by Sweeney. He is safer once out of the children's home, but he still sees Sweeney at school. He must still feel threatened because he takes the cheese knife, using it to threaten the would-be bike thief. In the wake of his mother's death, he is defending himself in the only way he can think of.

Alem also endures the formalised conflict of the court process, in which opposing lawyers argue over his case.

How does conflict lead to tragedy in the play?

First, Mrs Kelo is 'hacked to death' (Scene 18) as a result of the conflict between Ethiopia and Eritrea. This almost drives Alem to turn to violence himself. Ruth can see that there's 'a time-bomb strapped on the inside of him' (Scene 13). She feels that he could explode because he is under so much stress.

The second tragedy is the murder of Mr Kelo by Tewdros, who claims to be from the organisation EAST but clearly does not support its peaceful aims. He is presumably motivated by the conflict between Ethiopia and Eritrea, which EAST is trying to end, but Sissay leaves this open-ended.

What alternatives to conflict does the play suggest?

Mr Kelo wants peace: 'Remember to love your neighbours because peace is better than war, wherever you live' (Mr Kelo's letter: Scene 2). EAST promotes peace, although Mr Kelo finds that its London branch has been infiltrated by people like Tewdros.

Alem outlines the difficult process of achieving peace. He does not sound hopeful about Ethiopian and Eritrean politicians having the will to negotiate and sign a peace treaty. He sounds more hopeful that the younger generation will be able to create 'a culture of peace' (Scene 25).

Key Quotations to Learn

Alem [reading Mr Kelo's letter]: We just cannot afford to risk another attack. (Scene 2)

Sweeney [to Alem]: Say one bad word about my family again and I'll cut you up. (Scene 4)

Mr Kelo: Two men pass on the street are sworn enemies. (Scene 20)

Summary

- Mr Kelo leaves Alem in London so he will be safe from the conflict at home.
- Alem experiences violence in the children's home from Sweeney.
- When a youth tries to take his bike, Alem threatens him with violence.
- Mrs Kelo is murdered in Africa, her husband in London.
- Alem becomes a champion of peace.

Sample Analysis

The court process formalises conflict. The British legal system is **adversarial**: it attempts to reach a fair decision by having a prosecutor, or in Alem's case a lawyer acting for the government, arguing against a defence lawyer who argues on behalf of the asylum seeker. The judge hears both sides and reaches a decision. Mr Kelo has faith in this system, but Alem tells him, 'The judge doesn't know anything about Ethiopia or Eritrea', showing the lack of faith that makes him resort to a protest campaign.

Questions

QUICK TEST
1. What situation lies behind the inciting incident of this play?
2. What evidence is there that Alem still feels threatened when living with the Fitzgeralds?
3. Name the type of legal system in Britain, in which lawyers oppose each other.
4. Who says Alem has a 'time-bomb' inside him?
5. What will Ethiopia and Eritrea have to do before they can stop fighting?

EXAM PRACTICE
'The play presents a pessimistic view of human conflict.' Write a plan for an essay arguing for or against this statement.

Family and Friendship

You must be able to: write about the importance of family and friendship in the play.

How is the Kelo family shown positively?

The play's opening scene shows Alem's close relationship with his father when they discuss the stars. The conversation is extended in Scene 7, showing Alem's respect for his father. It is interesting that Alem never questions his father's decision to take him to London on the pretext of a holiday and then leave him there. In the children's home, Alem remains confident that his parents will fetch him, telling a sceptical Mustapha, 'Father and mother will be coming soon' (Scene 4).

How is the Fitzgerald family portrayed?

The Fitzgerald family are portrayed as kind, cooperative and keen to do some good in the world by fostering: 'if we can help someone else then we should' (Scene 11). There is no doubt of the love between Mr and Mrs Fitzgerald. Mr Fitzgerald compares his love for his wife to the stars, but adds, 'I just don't want you hurt' (Scene 11), because he worries about her becoming attached to Alem.

Ruth Fitzgerald is also supportive to Alem, saying he can trust her like a sister, and letting him sob in her arms after his mother dies.

How is family shown negatively?

The boys in the children's home are there because they cannot be with their families. The audience is left with the impression that the 'family reasons' mentioned by Mustapha are likely to mean, in effect, that the families are unable to look after the children – that one or both of the parents are absent, as in the case of Mustapha, or are actively abusive, as with Sweeney.

In Scene 4 we learn of Sweeney's negative attitude towards his family. Nonetheless, he attacks Alem supposedly because he thinks Alem is disrespecting his family: 'I said Are You Calling My Family Name?' It is only in Scene 15 that Sweeney reveals that his father used to beat him up, 'Every day.'

There is even a negative side to the way Alem's family relationships are shown when he and his father disagree over the anti-deportation campaign.

How are Alem's friendships shown?

Alem thinks Mustapha might not find it easy 'being around a family' if he comes back to the Fitzgerald house, showing his sensitivity to his friend's possible feelings. Mustapha says, 'Family's the friends you make,' then rephrases this: 'Friends are like the family you make' (Scene 10). This shows how important friends are to him – including Alem.

Mustapha lets Alem down as a friend by not helping him stand up to Sweeney, but he apologises and becomes a loyal friend. He and Ruth are good friends to Alem and help organise the anti-deportation campaign.

Key Quotations to Learn

Alem: And most of all we are separated from our families. (Scene 4)

Sweeney: You know what family does? Family messes you up. (Scene 4)

Alem: Father, why do you forsake me, break me, love and hate me? (Scene 20)

Summary

- Alem loves, respects and trusts his parents.
- The Fitzgeralds are a supportive surrogate family to Alem.
- Some boys in the children's home have negative experiences of family, especially Sweeney.
- Alem falls out with his father because he disapproves of Alem's campaign.
- Alem forms close friendships with Mustapha and Ruth.

Sample Analysis

As Alem becomes more independent and assimilated into London culture, his father objects to the way he now speaks. He objects even more to Alem's plans to protest against the asylum decision, and even raises his hand to hit him. This shows there can be clashes between the generations. In particular, parents may disapprove of their children's independent behaviour and try to hold them back. This may partly reflect a difference between family values in Ethiopia and the UK.

Questions

QUICK TEST
1. What do Alem and his father talk about in Scenes 1 and 7?
2. To what does Mr Fitzgerald compare his love for his wife?
3. Who thinks that 'family messes you up'?
4. Who finds support in friends rather than family?
5. How does Mr Kelo betray his peace-loving principles near the end of the play?

EXAM PRACTICE
Using one or more of the 'Key Quotations to Learn', write one or two paragraphs for an essay explaining how positively you think the play portrays family.

You must be able to: write about the link between identity and growing up in the play.

How are issues of identity at the heart of the play?

The soldiers demand to know Mr Kelo's nationality. They are not satisfied with the answer that he is African. It is the fact that Mr Kelo is Ethiopian and his wife Eritrean, making Alem 'a dirty poison, a mongrel' according to one soldier, that makes Mr Kelo take Alem to England.

Alem himself does not identify exclusively with one side or the other. Increasingly, however, he becomes assimilated into English life, speaking and behaving like his new friends.

How does Alem grow up and develop as a character?

Alem adapts to life with the Fitzgeralds, and is more secure with them than in the children's home, but he still feels unsafe. When he stands up to 'Hooded', he repeatedly demands that the youth should say his name, and not call him Refugee Boy. This symbolises him claiming his own identity.

Ironically, it is Sweeney who steers Alem away from identifying with the world of street violence, recognising that Alem is unsuited to it and that it is not a good life to lead.

How do other characters grow up and develop?

Mustapha begins the play being bullied by Sweeney. Later, he realises that although he was also being bullied, it was morally wrong of him to let Sweeney bully Alem. With this new maturity, he apologises: 'I'm sorry, man' (Scene 10).

In the same scene, Mustapha is also seen becoming more rebellious, telling Alem that he has poured paint over the children's home roof. Later, his rebelliousness is channelled constructively into the community protest.

Ruth also develops, gradually overcoming her ambivalence about Alem, honestly explaining her caution and becoming like his sister, and a good friend.

How does the play link growing up to identity?

For Alem, growing up involves owning his identity. He does not want to be seen merely as 'Refugee Boy', which he makes clear to the 'Hooded' youth. However, by the end of the play he acknowledges that this is part of his identity: 'I'm the refugee boy' (Scene 19).

Although Alem becomes assimilated into English culture, he realises that his African background is part of his identity. When he argues with his father, he points out that the judge knows nothing about Ethiopia or Eritrea. His standing up for this viewpoint shows that he is thinking for himself.

When he finally addresses the crowd, he points out that, in Amharic, 'Alem' means 'World', implying that he identifies with all humanity. His vision expands to encompass the ideal of world peace.

Key Quotations to Learn

Alem [to Hooded]: Do you know where I am from? Do you know what's happened to me? (Scene 15)

Alem [to his father]: I am older. I am grown. (Scene 20)

Alem [to the crowd]: And then my friends and I would travel anywhere in the world … (Scene 27)

Summary

- The soldiers cannot accept a mixed family; they demand to know Mr Kelo's nationality.
- Alem adapts to his new life and becomes assimilated into English society.
- Alem insists on being called by his real name, and almost follows a path of violence.
- Ruth and Mustapha also mature during the play.
- Alem comes to accept his background as part of his identity, but identifies with the world.

Sample Analysis

Alem has to adapt fast. First, he finds himself alone in the hotel, then he is living in a children's home and going to an English school. In the children's home, he is violently bullied. He tries to insist on being called Alem, not Ali, but he gives in to Sweeney and calls himself 'Refugee Boy'. This is very different from the novel, in which the boys fight when Sweeney demands his chips, and Alem defends himself. In the play, Sissay makes Sweeney a **catalyst** to Alem's growing up to choose peace over violence.

Questions

QUICK TEST
1. What does Mr Kelo call himself when soldiers demand to know his nationality?
2. Who steers Alem away from street violence?
3. Why does Alem claim that he and his father cannot rely on the judge's wisdom?
4. In what two ways does Mustapha show he is growing up?
5. What would Alem's ideal world be?

EXAM PRACTICE
Write one or two paragraphs comparing the development of teenage and adult characters in the play.

You must be able to: write about the roles played by UK law and the social care system in the play.

How is UK immigration law important to Alem and his father?

As Alem is only fourteen, as soon as Mr Hardwick calls 'the people', he becomes the responsibility of the UK Government because he has no adult to care for him in England. Whereas the novel shows Alem with people from the Refugee Council, the play jumps straight to where he is placed – a government-funded children's home. When he runs away, foster parents are found for him – the Fitzgeralds, whose expenses are paid by social services (a branch of government).

When Mr Kelo returns to England, he applies for asylum for himself and Alem. He must do this in order to be allowed to remain in the UK and to work and receive benefits such as access to healthcare. Otherwise he will be sent back to Ethiopia. Once Mr Kelo is in London, Alem is no longer an unaccompanied child, so he has to be granted asylum as well, or return with his father.

How does the social care system treat Alem?

At first, Alem is put into the children's home. Unfortunately, however good the staff are (and we never see them in the play), they cannot be a substitute for loving parents. It is also likely that some children will be in the home because of their dysfunctional families, as is likely to be the case with Sweeney. Some may therefore be insecure and may behave badly as a result – like Sweeney.

The system, however, serves Alem well when he is fostered by the Fitzgeralds, who are a kind, stable family who do their best to make him feel at home.

How does Alem take the law into his own hands?

When Alem is threatened by 'Hooded', he shows that he is prepared to take the law into his own hands. After all, the police are nowhere near, and even if he were to report his bike stolen, he would be unlikely to get it back.

He tackles the law more constructively after the asylum application has been refused. Mr Kelo has what could be called a naïve faith in British justice, but Alem does not share it. He sees the law as political, and decides to embrace the protest campaign in the hope that public pressure will influence the appeal.

Key Quotations to Learn

Mustapha [explaining why children are in the home]: Some for trials, some for family reasons. (Scene 4)

Mr Kelo [to Alem]: We should wait for the appeal. (Scene 20)

Alem: Everything is politics, Father! (Scene 20)

Summary

- Because of his age, Alem becomes the responsibility of the UK Government.
- He is placed in a children's home by social services. (In the novel, it is the Refugee Council that places him in the home with the approval of social services.)
- When Alem runs away from the children's home, social services find him good foster parents – the Fitzgeralds.
- Alem tries to protect himself illegally, with a knife, because he feels he has to.
- Mr Kelo has faith in the UK immigration system and the asylum appeal system; Alem feels they should put pressure on the Government by protesting.

Sample Analysis

The first hint that Alem does not feel he can rely on the protection of the law is when Mrs Fitzgerald notices that the cheese knife has gone. We discover later that Alem has taken it to protect himself. This is not so surprising, given that he has lived in two countries where his family has been threatened by soldiers who are paid by the state, and are therefore meant to uphold the law. He also doubts the fairness of the UK legal system, unlike his father.

Questions

QUICK TEST
1. Why must Mr Kelo apply for asylum?
2. What is the first clue that Alem feels he cannot rely on the law to protect him?
3. How has Alem's experience in Africa made him distrust the law?
4. What is Mr Kelo's attitude towards the UK legal system?
5. Why do Alem and his friends start a campaign?

EXAM PRACTICE
Write one or more paragraphs explaining how far you think the play shows the UK legal system as fair and effective.

You must be able to: understand how to approach the exam question and meet the requirements of the mark scheme.

Quick Tips

- You will get a choice of two questions, each based on a short quotation from the play. One is likely to be on a character, the other on a theme. You will be told to refer to the context of the play in your answer.

- The question will carry 40 marks, including 8 marks for using a range of appropriate vocabulary and sentence structures, and accurate spelling and punctuation.

- Make sure you know what the question is asking you. Underline key words. Consider how the question might be interpreted. For example, if you are asked about courage in the play, think of the many ways in which a character can show courage.

- You should spend about 50 minutes on your *Refugee Boy* response. Allow yourself between five and ten minutes to plan a well-structured answer.

- It can sometimes help, after each paragraph, to quickly reread the question to keep yourself focused on the exam task.

- Keep your writing concise. If you waste time 'waffling' – especially in a long introduction – you won't be able to include the depth of skills that the mark scheme requires.

- Refer to the context of the play, but don't write a long account of it. Keep what you say strictly relevant to elements of the plot, characters or themes.

- It is a good idea to remember what the mark scheme is asking of you ...

AO1: Understand and respond to the play (16 marks)

This is all about coming up with a range of points that match the question, interpreting and explaining the ideas of Zephaniah and Sissay, supporting these ideas with references from the play, and writing your essay in a mature, academic style.

Lower	Middle	Upper
The essay has some good ideas that are mostly relevant. Some quotations and references are used to support the ideas.	A clear essay that always focuses on the exam question. Quotations and references support ideas effectively. The response refers to the extract and to other points in the play.	A convincing, well-structured essay that answers the question fully. Quotations and references are well-chosen and integrated into sentences. The response covers the whole play (not everything, but ideas from the extract and a range of other scenes).

AO3: Understand the relationship between the play and its contexts (16 marks)

For this part of the mark scheme, you need to show your understanding of how the characters, plot or ideas in the play relate to its background – the conflict between Ethiopia and Eritrea, UK immigration law and social services, the authors' lives, and the fact that the play is based on the novel.

Lower	Middle	Upper
Some awareness of how ideas in the play link to its contexts.	References to relevant aspects of contexts show a clear understanding.	Exploration is linked to specific aspects of the play's contexts to show a detailed understanding. Context is fully integrated.

AO4: Written accuracy (8 marks)

You need to use a range of accurate vocabulary, punctuation and spelling in order to convey your ideas clearly and effectively.

Lower	Middle	Upper
Reasonable level of accuracy. Errors do not get in the way of the essay making sense.	Good level of accuracy. Vocabulary and sentences help to keep ideas clear.	Consistent high level of accuracy. Vocabulary and sentences are used to make ideas clear and precise.

1. Mr Kelo: Remember to love your neighbours because peace is better than war …
   - In what ways is Mr Kelo important in the play?
   - You **must** refer to the context of the play in your answer.

2. Sweeney: Your country don't want you and it don't want you because you're liars and thieves …
   - Explore the significance of Sweeney in *Refugee Boy*.
   - You **must** refer to the context of the play in your answer.

3. Alem: Damn right. I'm the refugee. I'm the boy. I'm the refugee boy.
   - In what ways does Alem develop in the play?
   - You **must** refer to the context of the play in your answer.

4. Alem: What's my name? My full name? Say my name.
   - Explore the importance of identity for Alem.
   - You **must** refer to the context of the play in your answer.

5. Alem: My family don't act like sinners. My father is a good man. And so is my mother.
   - Explore the importance of family to Alem.
   - You **must** refer to the context of the play in your answer.

6. Alem: In my homeland they are fighting over a border, a border that is mainly dust and rocks.
   - Explore the development of Alem as a peacemaker in the play.
   - You **must** refer to the context of the play in your answer.

7. Mustapha: Keep your head down and everything will be all right.
   - In what ways is Mustapha important in the play?
   - You **must** refer to the context of the play in your answer.

8. Mrs Fitzgerald: One day you'll have to do your own washing and then you might, you might understand.
   - Explain the significance of Mrs Fitzgerald in the play.
   - You **must** refer to the context of the play in your answer.

9. Mr Fitzgerald: You'll be right at home here, boy.
   - How is Mr Fitzgerald important in the play?
   - You **must** refer to the context of the play in your answer.

10. Mr Fitzgerald: See all the stars out there? Count them and times by as many and you won't get close to how much I love you. I'm lost here.
    - Explore the importance of the relationship between Mr and Mrs Fitzgerald.
    - You **must** refer to the context of the play in your answer.

11. Ruth: I wish I could take all those memories away for you.
    - Explore the relationship between Ruth and Alem.
    - You **must** refer to the context of the play in your answer.

12. Ruth: We've had like nine foster children here and sometimes they steal things and one time I was attacked in the middle of the night.
    - In what ways is Ruth important in the play?
    - You **must** refer to the context of the play in your answer.

13. Mustapha: Poured paint on the roof from the top window …
    - Explore the role of rebellion and dissent in the play.
    - You **must** refer to the context of the play in your answer.

14. Alem: Everything is politics, Father!
    - Explore the importance of politics in the play.
    - You **must** refer to the context of the play in your answer.

15. Sweeney: Used to beat me. Used to try and rearrange my face for me. Every day. Dad.
    - How is parenting presented in the play?
    - You **must** refer to the context of the play in your answer.

16. Mr Fitzgerald: You are part of our family.
    - How is family important in the play?
    - You **must** refer to the context of the play in your answer.

17. Soldier: Leave Ethiopia or die! Your choice, Mr Kelo.
    - Explore the significance of conflict in *Refugee Boy*.
    - You **must** refer to the context of the play in your answer.

18. Alem: I am older. I am grown.
    - Explore the importance of growing up in the play.
    - You **must** refer to the context of the play in your answer.

19. Mr Kelo: We should wait for the appeal.
    - Explore how the British legal and social care systems are presented in the play.
    - You **must** refer to the context of the play in your answer.

20. Mustapha: Friends are like the family you make.
    - Explore the importance of friendships in the play.
    - You **must** refer to the context of the play in your answer.

21. Sweeney: Nobody wants you. Not even the people who work here.
    - In what ways do concepts of home and belonging feature in the play?
    - You **must** refer to the context of the play in your answer.

22. Alem: Do you know where I am from? Do you know what's happened to me?
    - How are past experiences shown to be important in the play?
    - You **must** refer to the context of the play in your answer.

23. Alem: Father, why do you forsake me, break me, love and hate me?
    - Explore the importance of family conflict in *Refugee Boy*.
    - You **must** refer to the context of the play in your answer.

Planning a Character Question Response

You must be able to: understand what an exam question is asking you and prepare your response.

How might an exam question on character be phrased?

A typical character question will read like this:

> Sweeney: Your country don't want you and it don't want you because you're liars and thieves …
>
> • Explain the significance of Sweeney in *Refugee Boy*.
>
> • You **must** refer to the context of the play in your answer.
>   40 marks (includes 8 marks for the range of appropriate vocabulary and sentence structures, and accurate use of spelling and punctuation)

How do I work out what to do?

The focus of this question is clear: Sweeney's role in the play.

'Explain', 'significance' and 'context' are important elements of this question.

For AO1, these words show that you need to display a clear understanding of what Sweeney is like and how this relates to the themes of the play and the intentions of Zephaniah and Sissay.

For AO3, you need to link your interpretations to the play's social, historical or literary context.

You also need to remember to write in an accurate and sophisticated way to achieve your eight AO4 marks for spelling, punctuation, grammar and expression.

How can I plan my essay?

You have approximately 50 minutes to write your essay.

This isn't long but you should spend the first five minutes writing a quick plan. This will help you to focus your thoughts and produce a well-structured essay.

Try to come up with five or six ideas. Each of these ideas can then be written up as a paragraph.

You can plan in whatever way you find most useful. Some students like to make a quick list of points and then re-number them in a logical order. Spider diagrams are particularly popular; look at the example on the opposite page.

Does not seem dangerous at first. Invites Alem to play table tennis, and offers to teach him. However, he boasts about how he would 'thrash' Mustapha. Calls Alem 'Ali' and ignores his correction. Yet insists on his own name. This introduces the theme of identity.

You need a nickname, man.

My name is Sweeney. No nickname. It doesn't get shortened.

His violence is first shown when he says what he does to anyone who alters his name. Also hinted at by Mustapha's readiness to give him his chips. Becomes explicit when he attacks Alem, indicating the threat Alem faces in the children's home.

Gimme your chips, Musty.

If anyone calls me anything else but Sweeney I break their fingers and I slice them.

Claims Alem is insulting his family, subjects him to racist abuse, then attacks him and makes him call himself 'Refugee Boy'. This shows what Alem has to cope with in Britain. When Zephaniah's novel was published in 2001, less had been done officially to tackle racism.

I said Are You Calling My Family Name?

Your country don't want you and it don't want you because you're liars and thieves.

How Sweeney is significant

Surprisingly, defends Alem against bike mugger. Strokes Alem's face – a show of power or a hint that he finds Alem attractive? Helps to steer Alem away from violence.

You don't want to be like us, Alem.

You don't wanna get into knife fights.

Has negative view of family life. Confides in Alem that his father beat him up – explains his bullying.

Family messes you up.

Used to try and rearrange my face for me.

Summary

- Make sure you know what the focus of the essay is.
- Interpret the character: what does he represent and what ideas are conveyed?
- Try to relate your ideas to the play's context and the authors' intentions.

Questions

QUICK TEST
1. What key skills do you need to show in your answer?
2. What are the benefits of quickly planning your essay?
3. Why do you need to take care with your writing?

EXAM PRACTICE
Plan a response to the following exam question.
Sweeney: Hey, Ali. You two are spending a lot of time together lately.
Explore Sweeney's relationship with Alem and Mustapha.
You **must** refer to the context of the play in your answer.

Sweeney: Your country don't want you and it don't want you because you're liars and thieves …

- Explain the significance of Sweeney in *Refugee Boy*.
- You **must** refer to the context of the play in your answer.

[40 marks, including 8 AO4 marks]

Sweeney is important as a character because of the effect he has on Alem (1). He does not seem too bad at first, he just seems like he needs to be best at everything. 'I'd thrash you though.' He also insists on only being called Sweeney, even though he calls Mustapha 'Musty' and Alem 'Ali'. He wants to show that he is special, he wants respect (2).

He seems more obviously a bully when he tells Mustapha to give him his chips and Mustapha just hands them over without any complaint. 'Gimme your chips, Musty.' This shows that he is a typical bully (3). In a place like the children's home, he gets away with it because there are a lot of boys. It might be short-staffed and they cannot look out all the time. If anyone calls him anything else he will 'break their fingers and … slice them' (4).

When Sweeney says that family 'messes you up' and 'acts like sinners' this more or less forces Alem to stick up for his own family, so he does. 'My family don't act like sinners. My father is a good man. And so is my mother.' This shows how much Alem respects his own family, even though his father has left him alone in a hotel and that is why he is now in the children's home. This is because he is from a different culture (5).

Sweeney thinks that Alem is disrespecting his family. 'You talkin' bad about my family?' It is not really clear if he really thinks this or if he just wants an excuse to show Alem who is boss in the children's home (6). Mustapha does try to calm the situation down. He even dares to point out to Sweeney that it was his idea. 'You said it first, Sweeney.' Sweeney totally ignores this, which shows that he just wants to go on thinking Alem has offended him, or that he is just not a good listener.

He just tells Mustapha to shut up. Then he gets into an unacceptable racist rant about refugees. 'You're liars and thieves.' He talks insultingly about another refugee who killed himself. He calls him 'Tampax Tambo'. Perhaps Sweeney was why he did it (7). His attitude is typical of what a lot of people thought when Benjamin Zephaniah wrote the book. Sweeney even punches Alem and says 'I'll cut you up.' This shows what a lot of difficulty Alem faces wherever he goes because he is a refugee (8).

It is quite surprising when Sweeney later comes to Alem's rescue and makes the bike mugger back off (9). He even teases Alem about his cheese knife and strokes his face. This shows that Sweeney can be kind-hearted and has a sense of humour after all (10). We could even feel sorry for Sweeney because his father used to beat him up. 'Every day. Dad.' This shows Alem that even a bully is not all bad (11).

Sweeney is not the main character of the play 'Refugee Boy' but he is significant because he is part of Alem's learning journey (12).

1. Good starting sentence setting out the main argument. AO1

2. Good points and evidence, but the first quotation could be embedded, and explained. Also, 'he just seems' and 'he wants respect' should start new sentences or be preceded by semicolons. AO1/ AO4

3. A well-chosen quotation, though it would be better if it was embedded. The comment on it is too vague and does not directly relate to it. AO1

4. Good context, but next sentence does not quite follow on. AO1/AO3

5. Good point and evidence, but the comment on Alem needs to be tied in more closely to the question. Last sentence refers to context, but too simplistically. AO1/AO3

6. Good point, raising alternative interpretations. It would be better to embed the quotation and not to repeat 'really'. AO1

7. Speculation that needs to be justified by evidence to gain credit. AO1

8. Context, but could be explained and tied in more effectively. AO3

9. Good point, but could do with more analysis. AO1

10. Two good observations but they need more analysis. AO1

11. Important point, but the quotation could be better chosen, embedded and explained. AO1

12. A short but adequate conclusion making an interesting and relevant point. AO1

Questions

EXAM PRACTICE

Choose a paragraph from this essay. Read it through a few times then try to rewrite and improve it. You might:

- improve the sophistication of the language or the clarity of expression
- replace a reference with a quotation
- ensure quotations are embedded in the sentence
- provide a clearer or deeper interpretation of Sweeney's character
- link context to the interpretation more effectively.

A proportion of the best top-band answers will be awarded Grade 8 or Grade 9. To achieve this, you should aim for a sophisticated, fluent and nuanced response that displays flair and originality.

Sweeney: Your country don't want you and it don't want you because you're liars and thieves ...

- Explain the significance of Sweeney in *Refugee Boy*.
- You **must** refer to the context of the play in your answer.

[40 marks, including 8 AO4 marks]

Sweeney is significant because of his influence on Alem and the insights he provides into the social care system. He is the antagonist who challenges the protagonist, Alem, helping him to grow up – a device typical of Bildungsroman narratives (1).

At first, Sweeney seems harmless. He invites Mustapha and Alem to play table tennis, and even offers to teach Alem. However, he boasts about his table tennis, aggressively saying he will 'thrash' Mustapha, and even about his teaching: 'Best teacher, me.' He feels a need to be seen as the best at everything (2).

He becomes threatening when he insists that Alem should be renamed: 'You need a nickname, man.' He ignores Alem's resistance. He also shows that renaming is a show of power in his statement, 'My name is Sweeney. No nickname. It doesn't get shortened.' This relates to the theme of identity. It may be that in the absence of parents in the children's home, he feels a special need to insist on his identity as 'top dog' (3).

Sweeney suddenly seems dangerous when he says he will break the fingers of anyone changing his name, and 'slice them', hinting that he is capable of extreme violence. Mustapha handing over his chips is another clue. Mustapha must be frightened of Sweeney to do this, especially since he complains about not having enough chips (4).

The violence explodes when Sweeney claims that Alem is disrespecting his family, demanding, 'Are You Calling My Family Name?' He has just been saying that 'Family messes you up', so it is ironic that he now appears to be rejecting criticism of them (5). He launches into a racist anti-refugee rant against Alem. His line 'Your country don't want you ...' shows the kind of racist ignorance that Zephaniah and Sissay may have experienced when they were growing up in the 1980s. It shows what Alem has to cope with even after escaping the violent threat of the Ethiopian–Eritrean war, and what refugees must encounter even now (6).

When Sweeney demands that Alem call himself 'Refugee Boy', Alem tries to insist on his name – his individual identity – but eventually gives in to physical violence, at knifepoint. This traumatic incident makes him flee the home, which is why he is placed with foster parents (7).

Sweeney disappears from Zephaniah's novel after Alem leaves the home. Sissay enlarges his role, having him defend Alem against the bike mugger (8). Alem's violent reaction to the mugger seems like a continued reaction to Sweeney. He may have got the idea of the knife from him, and his repeated demands to the mugger, 'Say my name', makes it seem that the earlier incident has made him determined to defend his identity (9).

Sweeney's warning, 'You don't want to be like us, Alem', helps to steer him away from a path of violence, helping him to become a peacemaker. His line 'You don't wanna get into knife fights. Cut up that good smooth skin of yours' shows unexpected concern, but it also shows that Sweeney can see Alem is not cut out for a life of violence. Sweeney's gesture of stroking Alem's face seems oddly tender. It could be a sinister display of power, showing he can get away with it, or Sweeney may be attracted to Alem (10).

It is also surprising that Sweeney, so intent on appearing tough, confides that his father used to 'try and rearrange' his face. This bitter humour about parental abuse hints at why Sweeney is in the children's home, like many young people in the social care system, and why he became a bully. However, his experience means he can now influence Alem for the good (11).

1. Short but effective introduction, mapping out the main argument of the response and referring to context. AO1/AO3
2. Shows development of character with two well-chosen quotations as evidence, explaining their significance. AO1
3. Links quotations and explains them, referring to context. AO1/AO3
4. Uses a close reference to the text as evidence and explains its significance. AO1
5. A perceptive comment on the impact of the text. AO1
6. Detailed reference to historical, biographical and topical context. AO3
7. Explains the impact on Alem and relates the incident to identity. It could perhaps explain more clearly how this benefits Alem. AO1
8. Awareness of the context of the adaptation. AO3
9. Sophisticated interpretation tracking Sweeney's role in Alem's development. AO1
10. Develops the argument of the essay. Sophisticated presentation of possible interpretations. AO1
11. A fluent paragraph combining evidence, analysis and context. AO1/AO3

Questions

EXAM PRACTICE

Spend 50 minutes writing an answer to the following question:

Sweeney: Hey, Ali. You two are spending a lot of time together lately.

Explore Sweeney's relationship with Alem and Mustapha.

You **must** refer to the context of the play in your answer.

Remember to use the plan you have already prepared.

Planning a Theme Question Response

You must be able to: understand what an exam question is asking you and prepare your response.

How might an exam question on a theme be phrased?

A typical theme question will read like this:

Alem [reading Mr Kelo's letter]: We just cannot afford to risk another attack.
- Explore the importance of conflict in the play.
- You **must** refer to the context of the play in your answer.

[40 marks, including 8 AO4 marks]

How do I work out what to do?

The focus of this question is clear: how conflict features in the play.

'Explore', 'importance' and 'conflict' are important elements of this question.

For AO1, these words show that you need to display a clear understanding of what conflicts there are in the play and how these relate to the themes of the play and the authors' intentions.

For AO3, you need to link your interpretations to the play's social, historical or literary context.

You also need to remember to write in an accurate and sophisticated way to achieve your eight AO4 marks for spelling, punctuation, grammar and expression.

How can I plan my essay?

You have approximately 50 minutes to write your essay.

This isn't long but you should spend the first five minutes writing a quick plan. This will help you to focus your thoughts and produce a well-structured essay.

Try to come up with five or six ideas. Each of these ideas can then be written up as a paragraph.

You can plan in whatever way you find most useful. Some students like to make a quick list of points and then re-number them in a logical order. Spider diagrams are particularly popular; look at the example on the opposite page.

The plot is set in motion by the Ethiopian–Eritrean conflict which leads to the dual-nationality Kelo family's persecution in both countries. The countries were at war 1961–91. Alem's birthplace, Badme, was hotly disputed. Full-scale war returned in 1998. Zephaniah's novel was published in 2001.

Alem: ... they are fighting over ... a border that is mainly dust and rocks.

The conflict is represented in two flashback scenes, set in Ethiopia, then Eritrea, in which soldiers break into the family home, call them traitors, call Alem a 'mongrel', and threaten their lives. Mr Kelo continues to work for peace through EAST. He hopes to bring Alem back from England, but gives up when his wife is murdered.

Soldier: ... like a hyena picking and choosing where he steals his next meal from.
Soldier: Dirty dog traitors.

Alem still faces violence in England. First, Sweeney racially abuses and attacks him. Then another boy tries to take his bike. Alem shows he is starting to think he must meet violence with violence, defending himself with a knife. Sweeney steers him away from this path – in the play but not the novel.

Sweeney: Same things gonna happen to you as happen to that other one boy ...
Sweeney: Take the knife and put it back where you got it ...

Importance of conflict

The asylum process is formalised conflict. The UK legal system is adversarial, aiming to reach a decision by lawyers arguing for and against Alem and his father's asylum. Mr Kelo trusts it, Alem doesn't. Alem chooses opposition by peaceful protest.

Mr Fitzgerald [as lawyer]: Most of the people in Ethiopia and Eritrea have not seen any fighting whatsoever.

Conflict exists even in loving families. Mr Kelo almost hits Alem because his background has conditioned him to see Alem disagreeing with him as disrespect. Ruth has differences of opinion with her parents, but they discuss them. The play shows that peaceful negotiation is better than violence.

Mr Kelo: Get out of my house!
Alem: We must become that new generation of peacemakers.

Summary

- Make sure you know what the focus of the essay is.
- Remember to interpret the theme: how is it shown and what ideas are being conveyed?
- Try to relate your ideas to the play's context and the authors' intentions.

Questions

QUICK TEST

1. What key skills do you need to show in your answer?
2. What are the benefits of quickly planning your essay?
3. Why do you need to take care with your writing?

EXAM PRACTICE

Plan a response to the following exam question.

Mrs Fitzgerald [as judge]: I must turn down your application for asylum.

Explore the importance of the law in *Refugee Boy*. You **must** refer to the context of the play in your answer. [40 marks, including 8 AO4 marks]

Alem [reading Mr Kelo's letter]: We just cannot afford to risk another attack.

- Explore the importance of conflict in the play.
- You **must** refer to the context of the play in your answer.

[40 marks, including 8 AO4 marks]

Alem is left in London for his safety by his dad because there is a war going on between Ethiopia and Eritrea (1). Alem calls this 'fighting over … a border that is mainly dust and rocks.' This shows how pointless it is (2). The countries are next to each other and Badme where Alem comes from is right on the border. He is half Ethiopian half Eritrean, so the family gets death threats from armed soldiers in both countries, wherever they go. Mr Kelo thinks Alem will be safe in England, so he brings him here and leaves him in the hotel (3). The author himself is of Ethiopian and Eritrean parentage so he would know what it is like (4).

The war is shown in two flashback scenes that are very similar but in the different countries. In both, soldiers break in and call the family 'dirty dog traitors'. One accuses Mr Kelo. 'You choose your homeland like a hyena picking and choosing where he steals his next meal from.' This shows he thinks Mr Kelo should just decide on one country and stay there and not be a scavenger like a hyena. Even in London Mr Kelo cannot escape the conflict, he is murdered by a man called Tewdros who objects to Alem's protest. 'Alem is gaining too much attention.' He probably wants the war to continue (5).

Even in England Alem is not safe. In the children's home he meets the bully Sweeney who seems friendly at first, asking him to play table tennis, but then gives him racial abuse 'you're all poison', and punches him. He is like the soldiers, threatening Alem. 'Same things gonna happen to you as happen to that other one boy.' (6) He also threatens to cut him up with a knife. This is what makes Alem try to do the same with the bike mugger. Luckily Sweeney tells him that he is not suited to violence and says he should 'Take the knife and put it back where you got it.' (7)

Even the British asylum process is a kind of conflict. One lawyer argues for the person to be sent back, the other argues for him being allowed to stay. In the play the judge hears both arguments and decides to send Alem and his father back because he thinks it is safe in Ethiopia and most people 'have not seen any fighting'. Mr Kelo puts his trust in the judge but Alem thinks they can't rely on this because he knows nothing about Ethiopia (8).

This shows us that conflict exists even in loving families (9). Mr Kelo is a typical Ethiopian father who thinks Alem should obey him, so he hits him when he argues with him about the protest (10). He even says, 'Get out of my house!', which shows he wants to throw Alem out (11). Even the loving Fitzgerald family have arguments over Themba and Alem.

Alem chooses non-violent protest in the end. The play's message is that like Mr Kelo says we should all, 'Love your neighbours because peace is better than war, wherever you live' (12).

1. 'Dad' is too informal a word choice, and 'conflict' would be more accurate than 'war'. AO1/AO3

2. A well-chosen quotation, simply embedded, but it would be better to say that this is Alem's view. AO1

3. Begins to retell the story. Punctuation could be improved. AO1/AO4

4. Context, but the statement is too vague and needs to be better integrated. AO3

5. A fairly sound paragraph with appropriate quotations, though only one is embedded; analysis could be more sophisticated, and punctuation could be improved. AO1/AO4

6. A simple but fairly effective comparison. The quotations could be analysed in more depth. AO1

7. Good observation and a well-chosen quotation, but it needs some analysis. AO1

8. A fairly sound paragraph with effective context. It would be more accurate to say Mr Kelo trusts the 'legal system'. AO1/ AO4

9. A good point. AO1

10. Legitimate context, but a more tentative wording, avoiding the idea of the 'typical Ethiopian father' would be better, and 'hits' is inaccurate. AO1/AO3

11. A well-chosen quotation but it needs closer analysis: as Alem says, it is not Mr Kelo's house. AO1

12. Effective use of a quotation to conclude, but the paragraph could be more fluently worded. AO1

Questions

Choose a paragraph from this essay. Read it through a few times then try to rewrite and improve it. You might:
* improve the sophistication of the language or the clarity of expression
* replace or supplement a reference with a quotation
* ensure quotations are embedded in the sentence
* provide alternative interpretations
* provide more context and link it to the interpretation more effectively.

Grade 7+ Annotated Response

A proportion of the best top-band answers will be awarded Grade 8 or Grade 9. To achieve this, you should aim for a sophisticated, fluent and nuanced response that displays flair and originality.

Alem [reading Mr Kelo's letter]: We just cannot afford to risk another attack.

- Explore the importance of conflict in the play.
- You **must** refer to the context of the play in your answer.

[40 marks, including 8 AO4 marks]

Conflict is at the heart of the play. Its inciting incident is Mr Kelo leaving Alem alone in a London hotel in order to keep him from the threat posed by the longstanding and ongoing conflict between neighbouring Ethiopia and Eritrea (1). In 1998, just three years before the publication of Zephaniah's novel, on which the play is based, this became a full-out war. The town Alem comes from, Badme, was on the border and therefore much disputed (2). As Alem calmly and impartially says, 'Some people think this area is part of Ethiopia and some people think this area is part of Eritrea.' He personally thinks that 'fighting over ... a border that is mainly dust and rocks' is pointless. The audience is left with this as the play's viewpoint, as no other character questions it (3).

The nature of the conflict is represented in two flashback scenes, one in each country, in which young soldiers break into the family's home and threaten them with ultimatums to leave that country 'or die'. The Ethiopian soldier is known to the family, showing how a border conflict turns neighbours against each other (4).

Key to the family's plight is the fact that Mr Kelo is Ethiopian, his wife Eritrean. Both soldiers think a mixed marriage is a betrayal and Alem is a 'mongrel', which dismisses him as a dog. The Eritrean soldier seems to want to blame Mr Kelo for the deaths of his comrades: 'You know how many have died while you were in Ethiopia?' He calls Mr Kelo a 'hyena', indicating his disgust for him (5).

Similar racist prejudice and disgust are shown by Sweeney, the bully who abuses and attacks Alem on the pretext of claiming Alem is insulting his family (6). It is likely that the playwright, Sissay, was influenced in his characterisation by his own experience in children's homes after being given up by his Ethiopian mother (7). Like the soldiers and other racists, Sweeney makes casually sweeping statements dismissing all refugees as 'liars and thieves ... poison'. When he assaults Alem and threatens him with a knife, it seems, ironically, that Alem is little better off in England than Africa (8).

There is a key difference, however, in Sweeney's role in Zephaniah's novel and in the play. In the latter, he goes on to defend Alem from the bike mugger and to discourage him from pursuing a life of street violence. He teases him about his cheese knife, recognising that Alem is not really cut out for 'knife fights'. This helps to turn Alem away from violence towards peaceful protest as a better alternative (9).

Alem experiences a more formal type of conflict in the UK legal system, which is adversarial, with the aim being that lawyers argue for and against a case. With an asylum application, one side argues that the applicant would be in danger if sent home, the other that they would be safe. In Alem's case, the lawyer for the Secretary of State considers that 'the risk to the lives of the appellants is minimal', the abstract language emphasising the depersonalising process (10).

The play also shows that conflict exists even within loving families. The Fitzgeralds argue about foster children, and Alem argues with his father about the asylum process. Perhaps reflecting his cultural background, Mr Kelo is outraged when Alem argues with him about the protest campaign. It is also a generational issue: Mr Kelo has a naïve faith in the UK legal system, while Alem sees it as out of touch with the real situation of refugees (11).

The ultimate message of the play, however, is that Mr Kelo was right when he wrote that 'peace is better than war, wherever you live'. Alem shows that he agrees by finally urging the younger generation to create 'a culture of peace' (12).

1. Concisely and fluently explains the key importance of conflict, referring correctly to what sets the plot in motion; good use of sentence types. AO1/AO4

2. Well integrated historical and literary context. AO3

3. Well-chosen quotations with insightful analysis. AO1

4. Develops the analysis of conflict using reference and a short, embedded quotation. AO1

5. Well-chosen embedded quotations with analysis. AO1

6. Fluent transition from one paragraph to the next, linking soldiers to Sweeney. AO1

7. Valid and integrated context. AO3

8. Effectively continues the comparison between the soldiers and Sweeney, using an embedded quotation. AO1

9. A well-handled transition using the link word 'however' and analysing how Sweeney influences Alem, thereby exploring how the play's treatment of conflict develops. AO1

10. Good integrated context and language analysis. AO1/AO3

11. Sensitive reference to context and a good insight into Mr Kelo and Alem. AO1/AO3

12. Effective conclusion with well-chosen embedded quotations. AO1

 ## Questions

EXAM PRACTICE
Spend 50 minutes writing an answer to the following question:
Mrs Fitzgerald [as judge]: I must turn down your application for asylum.
Explore the importance of the law in *Refugee Boy*.
You **must** refer to the context of the play in your answer.
[40 marks, including 8 AO4 marks]
Remember to use the plan you have already prepared.

Glossary

Acronym – an abbreviation consisting of initials that spell out a pronounceable word, such as EAST.

Adversarial – based on a contest between opposing factions.

Ambiguous – open to more than one interpretation (noun 'ambiguity').

Antagonist – character directly opposed to or threatening the main character; in *Refugee Boy*, this could be seen as Sweeney.

Assimilated – describing someone who becomes integrated with the customs and values of a different culture.

Asylum – refuge, a place of safety, or the legal status of a refugee guaranteed it by a government.

Bildungsroman – a novel focusing on how the protagonist grows up, or 'comes of age'.

Catalyst – an event or character responsible for bringing about an important change in another character or situation.

Chronological – the normal linear order in which time progresses.

Cliffhanger – a plot device by which the audience is left wanting to know what happens next, especially when an important character is at a **crisis point**.

Climax – the most important and exciting part of a narrative, usually near the end – in *Refugee Boy*, the death of Mr Kelo.

Colloquial – referring to popularly used informal language, including slang.

Crisis point – the point of highest danger, when key characters have the most to gain or lose – in *Refugee Boy* this could be Alem's confrontation with the bike mugger.

Device – a literary or dramatic technique intended to have a particular effect.

Dialogue – conversation between two or more characters.

Dramatic irony – a situation in which one person on stage has important information that is shared by the audience but not known to any other character on stage.

Expressionistic – using symbolism and distortion to express emotions and ideas rather than realism.

Flashback – a section of narrative that jumps back in time.

Foreshadowing – literary technique in which a story hints at future events.

Foster – a system in which adults (foster parents) care for children who cannot be with their parents, usually on a temporary basis (though it could lead to adoption).

Inciting incident – the key event that sets a narrative in motion.

Juxtaposed – placed next to or in contrast with something else, such as a dramatic scene.

Minor – in England a person under the age of 18.

Monologue – a speech given by a single character on stage as if thinking aloud, or addressing the audience.

Myth – an ancient story with symbolic meaning, passed on and developed over generations.

Narrative – story, or relating to a story.

Non-linear – not in normal chronological order.

Protagonist – the leading character in a play or novel, usually the one the audience or reader is encouraged to empathise with the most.

Social services – the branch of government responsible for the care of vulnerable children or adults, including supervision of children's homes and fostering.

Stage direction – an instruction in a play script telling actors what to do or how to speak.

Symbolic – having a meaning beyond the obvious literal one, in which an act or thing represents or suggests something else.

Tragic – relating to tragedy, a dramatic genre involving the death of a noble hero or heroine through fate or a character flaw. More generally, an extremely sad event, usually a death.

Ward of court – a child placed under the legal guardianship of the High Court, part of the UK's system of civil (non-criminal) law.

Answers

Pages 4–5

Quick Test

1. They take it in turns to shine.
2. In a London hotel room.
3. Cars
4. **Colloquial** speech – street language
5. Say 'I am a Refugee Boy'.

Exam Practice

Answers might include: Alem has had to cope with finding himself alone in a locked London hotel room and being questioned by the manager. Alem has learned that his father has gone back to Africa and left him alone in England. He has also had to get used to life in a children's home without his parents. He has been racially abused, punched and threatened at knife-point by Sweeney and forced to say 'I am a Refugee Boy'.

Pages 6–7

Quick Test

1. Eritrean
2. He helps him find his wallet by fetching his coat.
3. Themba
4. He is told he must go to court to be allowed to stay in England, but he doesn't want to stay.
5. Crying

Exam Practice

Answers might include: He has made friends with Mustapha, who has started to teach him colloquial English. He has escaped the children's home, where he was bullied, and been placed with kind-hearted foster parents – the Fitzgeralds.

Pages 8–9

Quick Test

1. Six
2. For pouring paint over the children's home roof.
3. Because they think she will become attached to Alem and then be upset when he leaves.
4. Five pounds
5. An Eritrean soldier

Exam Practice

Answers might include: The audience will at first wonder what could be in the letter – as will the Fitzgeralds. The audience will then sympathise with Alem receiving this shocking news in a letter. There is dramatic irony in the fact that the scene will be acted so that only Alem and the audience know that Mrs Kelo has been murdered. A dramatic device is used: the Fitzgeralds are present but not aware of Alem reading aloud. They will, therefore, be worried and baffled by his reaction.

Pages 10–11

Quick Test

1. Themba
2. She was in love with him.
3. Snow
4. Sweeney tells Alem to put the knife back where it came from and not get into knife fights.

5. He exaggerates the story, saying he was confronted by a whole gang of boys. He also makes up details of horrors he has seen in Africa, claiming he told the gang about these. He does not mention Sweeney's intervention.

Exam Practice

Answers might include: Alem has settled in with the Fitzgeralds and has learned to trust Ruth, and perhaps to find her attractive. He has also become more assertive since letting Sweeney force him to call himself 'Refugee Boy'. This seems to have made him angry and prepared to use violence to defend himself.

Pages 12–13

Quick Test

1. Alem is now a ward of court. There are legal proceedings to follow before he can be returned to his father's care.
2. He hears in court that his mother has been 'hacked to death'.
3. The adjudicator rules that Alem and his father would be in very little danger if they returned to Africa, because there is only a limited border conflict between Ethiopia and Eritrea.
4. Ruth
5. They plan a poster, leaflets, radio publicity, collecting money and a band.

Exam Practice

Answers might include: The lawyer speaking for the Secretary of State argues that there is no real war going on between Ethiopia and Eritrea, just a series of skirmishes over the border, and that if Alem and his father move back and live somewhere away from the border they will be safe. The lawyer for the Kelos argues that there has recently been a 'massive escalation' of the conflict, and that the Kelos are in danger in both countries because of being a 'mixed race' family.

Pages 14–15

Quick Test

1. He thinks they should wait quietly and patiently for the appeal.
2. Betraying the memory of Mrs Kelo, who 'was a fighter and would not stay quiet'.
3. By shortening the scenes and switching rapidly between the campaign and Mr Kelo.
4. Mustapha
5. EAST (The East African Solidarity Trust)

Exam Practice

Answers might include: Mr Kelo does not like the way Alem now speaks, which reflects his assimilation into teenage London life. For example, he insists on being called 'Father', which denotes more respect than the casual 'Dad'. Worse, he is outraged when Alem dares to argue with him about the asylum application. Mr Kelo thinks they should trust British justice and obey the judge; Alem does not share his faith, and wants to mount the protest campaign.

Pages 16–17

Quick Test

1. Dust and rocks

2. He says Alem is 'gaining too much attention'.
3. He wants his father to come up and introduce himself.
4. The respect of many young people in east London.
5. Alem now speaks the lines about the North Star that were previously his father's.

Exam Practice

Answers might include: Alem has matured and become more independent. He still loves and respects his father, as shown when he wants him to introduce himself to the crowd, but he goes ahead with the campaign, against his father's wishes. He seems to have renounced the violence he was beginning to embrace when he resisted the bike mugger, and to have become an effective spokesman for peace.

Pages 18–19

Quick Test
1. A novel about a young person growing up.
2. He is forced to become independent and discover his own individuality.
3. Mustapha and Ruth
4. This is the point at which Alem seems to have chosen the path of violence but is persuaded away from it by Sweeney.
5. They speed up the action and make it seem more urgent.

Exam Practice

A storyline might include: Alem waking in the hotel room; Alem being attacked by Sweeney; Alem hearing that his mother has died; the rejection of the asylum application; Alem addressing the crowd; the murder of Mr Kelo.

Pages 20–21

Quick Test
1. Birmingham
2. His mother was Ethiopian, his father Eritrean. He was given to foster parents in the UK, then put in a children's home.
3. The novel
4. Alem takes it from the Fitzgeralds' kitchen to defend himself. He threatens the bike mugger with it.
5. By the Fitzgeralds

Exam Practice

Answers might include: Zephaniah was born of Afro-Caribbean immigrant parents in 1958, and experienced racial prejudice. He served a prison sentence, so would be familiar with the courtroom setting. He has also visited many refugee camps and heard refugees' life stories. Sissay knows what it is to have Ethiopian and Eritrean parents, to be fostered by a white family, and what life is like in children's homes.

Pages 22–23

Quick Test
1. Waking up alone in the hotel room and being questioned by the manager.
2. Getting too few chips
3. On the street (by a bus stop)
4. The Kelos' homes in Ethiopia and Eritrea
5. Not at all

Exam Practice

Sample answer: The Fitzgerald family home is a fairly safe and comfortable place – certainly compared with the children's home. The Fitzgeralds make Alem welcome, though Ruth admits to having reasons to be cautious about him. However, there is some conflict and unease, particularly because of the family's experience with Alem's predecessor, Themba, who

took his own life. Mrs Fitzgerald feels unable to discuss this: 'I can't talk about Themba.' This shows that her approach is to try to ignore difficult feelings, whereas Ruth thinks they should discuss them.

Pages 24–25

Quick Test
1. Ethiopia
2. Badme
3. He is half-Ethiopian, half-Eritrean.
4. East African Solidarity Trust
5. That the Kelos could live safely in Africa.

Exam Practice

Sample answer: The family is persecuted in both Ethiopia and Eritrea because Mr Kelo is Ethiopian and his wife is Eritrean. Soldiers in both countries call him a traitor. An Eritrean soldier says he is like 'a hyena picking and choosing where he steals his next meal from', implying that Mr Kelo has no loyalty to either country and just wants to exploit both.

Although the family is clearly in danger in Ethiopia and Eritrea, the lawyer for the Secretary of State argues that most areas of both countries are at peace, and the family would be able to live safely there. The adjudicator believes this and therefore turns down their asylum application.

Pages 26–27

Quick Test
1. Their fear of persecution in their home country.
2. He wants Alem to rejoin him and Mrs Kelo in Africa when it is safe.
3. It is only legally possible to apply for asylum in the UK from within the UK.
4. He thinks they should obey the judge and go back to Africa.
5. Alem says the judge has no knowledge of life in Ethiopia or Eritrea.

Exam Practice

Answers might include: The Kelos have received death threats in Ethiopia and Eritrea, and they feel that they and Alem are still in danger there: 'This is a family that is in fear for their lives.' However, in order to apply for asylum in the UK, Mr Kelo and Alem must actually be in the UK. He therefore takes the risky step of coming to the UK on a tourist visa and leaving Alem here, knowing that the state will have to care for him. When he returns and applies for asylum, it is refused because the judge rules that Mr Kelo and Alem can safely return to Africa.

Pages 28–29

Quick Test
1. Sweeney
2. Social services
3. Mustapha
4. He tells her he hears her at night crying over Themba.
5. The actors playing the Fitzgeralds assume the roles of the lawyer and judge.

Exam Practice

Answers might include: In the children's home, Alem was racially abused and bullied by Sweeney. When Alem lives with the Fitzgeralds, he will still see Sweeney at school, but will see less of him than before, so he is safer. The Fitzgeralds are kind-hearted adults who are experienced foster parents and who care about Alem's welfare. He also forms a warm friendship with Ruth.

Quick Test

1. He says he didn't want his chips and was offering them to Mustapha.
2. His own parents.
3. It is about an orphan who has to find, or form, his own identity.
4. A cheese knife
5. Alem wants to mount an anti-deportation campaign. Mr Kelo strongly disagrees, saying they should not 'make a fuss' about their asylum application. Alem goes ahead with the campaign.

Exam Practice

Sample answer: At the start of the play, Alem is dependent on his father, and is very anxious when Mr Kelo leaves him alone in the hotel room. While in the children's home, he is bullied by Sweeney, and forced to call himself 'Refugee Boy'. After this experience he starts to carry a knife for self-defence – albeit a cheese knife. He seems to be turning to violence when he reacts violently to the bike mugger. He also insists on his identity: 'What's my name? My full name? Say my name.' However, Sweeney teases him and advises him against knife fights. This helps to return Alem to non-violence.

By the time of the asylum rejection, Alem has become more confident and independent, and defies his father by carrying on with the anti-deportation campaign. By the end of the play, he is an assertive peace campaigner.

Pages 32–33
Quick Test

1. A holiday
2. The murder of Mrs Kelo
3. By arguing with him about the anti-deportation campaign.
4. Dickens and Shakespeare
5. It is full of spies.

Exam Practice

Sample answer: Mr Kelo plans to leave Alem in London until it is safe for the family in Ethiopia or Eritrea. He and his wife have decided on this because 'We value [Alem's] life more than anything.' However, Mrs Kelo is murdered and this makes him return to London. Now he has to apply for asylum. Alem is no longer an unaccompanied minor, so if their appeal fails he will have to return to Africa with his father. In the meantime, EAST has been infiltrated by spies, one of whom murders him. Despite the fact that Mr Kelo and his wife 'gave everything to the cause of peace', he is killed by someone who evidently wants war.

Pages 34–35
Quick Test

1. Mustapha
2. Car mechanic
3. 'I am a Refugee Boy.'
4. He is put on curfew.
5. He helps organise the protest.

Exam Practice

Answers might include: 1 Mustapha befriends Alem in the home, gives him advice on survival there, and teaches him street slang. 2 He does appear to betray Alem when Sweeney attacks him, but Mustapha is afraid of Sweeney himself. 3 Despite his fear, he does make an effort to calm Sweeney down. When he tells Alem to call himself a 'Refugee Boy', this is to stop Sweeney hurting him. 5 Later, he apologises and they return to their friendship. 5 Mustapha supports Alem emotionally when his mother dies. 6 Mustapha helps Alem

and Ruth with the protest campaign, and speaks at it, calling himself Alem's 'best friend'.

Pages 36–37
Quick Test

1. Table tennis
2. A nickname – Ali
3. Sweeney
4. He orders the bike mugger to leave Alem alone.
5. Sweeney was regularly beaten by his father.

Exam Practice

Answers might include: Sweeney seems like the classic bully. He insists on being seen as the best at everything; he changes other boys' names but threatens to 'slice' anyone who alters his own; and he abuses and attacks Alem for no real reason. On the other hand, he turns up at the right moment and defends Alem from the bike mugger, advising Alem against getting into violence: 'You don't wanna get into knife fights.' He may even find Alem attractive, as he strokes his face – an unusually tender gesture for a bully in a boys' home.

Pages 38–39
Quick Test

1. The cheese knife
2. Bring her washing down
3. Truthfully
4. Ruth says they should talk about Themba.
5. Ireland

Exam Practice

Answers might include: She is under stress because she has not got over the experience of getting attached to a previous foster child, Themba, who then took his own life. Despite this, she has urged her husband to take on Alem. She is also running a household. She shows stress by snapping at Ruth and being unable to discuss Themba.

Pages 40–41
Quick Test

1. His wallet
2. He worries that his wife will become attached to him and be upset when he leaves.
3. He dislikes it.
4. He compares it to the number of stars in the sky.
5. He asks her to go and check that Alem is all right.

Exam Practice

Answers might include: Mr Fitzgerald is a caring man who agrees with his wife that if they can help someone by fostering, then they should. His kindness is clear when he tells Alem, 'You are part of our family.' However, it is not long since they fostered Themba, who took his own life, and he is afraid that his wife will become emotionally attached to Alem, as she did to Themba, and then get upset when he leaves. This is why he says, 'He's got to go home.'

Pages 42–43
Quick Test

1. Mustapha
2. 'Oliver'
3. Her father
4. He took his own life.
5. She is the project-leader.

Exam Practice

Answers might include: Her relationship with Alem is complicated by the fairly recent loss of Themba: 'One I fell for. He died.' She is still grieving him, as shown by her crying about him at night. Believing in openness, she tells Alem about her reasons for feeling cautious about letting him into her life. Nonetheless she allows herself to comfort Alem, telling him he can trust her like a sister. Her growing feelings for him are shown by her telling him, 'I wish I could take all those memories away for you' when he exaggerates the awful things he has seen in Africa.

Pages 44–45
Quick Test
1. He is joking about Alem making a lot of noise.
2. Ethiopia
3. He has clothes and shoes and is 'well fed'.
4. The deaths of his fellow Eritreans.
5. EAST – the East African Solidarity Trust

Exam Practice
Answers might include: The scenes show vividly that the Kelo family are in great danger whether in Ethiopia or Eritrea. They also show the prejudice of one group towards another, and the way that, in a border conflict, people are liable to seek revenge. Presenting the scenes as flashbacks also implies that the trauma of these episodes still affects Alem.

Pages 46–47
Quick Test
1. Asmara, in Eritrea
2. Amharic
3. Colloquial young people's English
4. World
5. He has a playful exchange of insults with Mustapha using 'street' language.

Exam Practice
Answers might include: 1 Belonging is certainly important. Mr Kelo brings Alem to England because his life is in danger in Ethiopia and Eritrea. Local people, represented by the soldiers in two scenes, do not think the Kelos belong in either country. 2 Sweeney, in his irrational racist rant, tells Alem that he does not belong in England – or anywhere. 3 The Fitzgeralds accept Alem as part of the family. 4 The protest campaign against the asylum rejection argues that the Kelos belong in Britain. 5 Other themes, such as conflict and family, are important, but they relate to belonging.

Pages 48–49
Quick Test
1. The conflict between Ethiopia and Eritrea, and the persecution of the Kelos in both countries.
2. He takes a cheese knife to defend himself.
3. Adversarial
4. Ruth
5. Negotiate and sign a peace treaty

Exam Practice
Answers might include: 1 The Ethiopian–Eritrean conflict has gone on for decades. 2 The attitudes of the soldiers in the two flashback scenes show the bitter feelings and desire for revenge that help to fuel the conflict. 3 Sweeney's racism shows how some people in Britain feel towards incomers, which fuels more conflict. 4 Mr Kelo is murdered by a man supposedly from an organisation formed to promote peace. 5 On the other hand, Sweeney helps to turn Alem against violence as a means of resolving conflict. 6 Alem becomes a respected peacemaker and is optimistic about peace.

Pages 50–51
Quick Test
1. The stars
2. The stars
3. Sweeney
4. Mustapha
5. He raises his hand to hit Alem.

Exam Practice
Answers might include: Alem tells Sweeney and Mustapha that the worst thing about being in the children's home is that 'we are separated from our families'. This shows family in a positive light. It is also significant that Alem never questions his father's decision to leave him alone in London. He respects him, even when he argues with him over the protest campaign. Alem also has a positive experience of a surrogate family with the Fitzgeralds. Sweeney and Mustapha present negative views of family, but this reflects their own dysfunctional experiences.

Pages 52–53
Quick Test
1. African
2. Sweeney
3. Because the judge knows nothing about Ethiopia or Eritrea.
4. He apologises to Alem for not doing more to stop Sweeney's bullying. He channels his rebelliousness into the anti-deportation campaign.
5. One in which everyone lived in peace.

Exam Practice
Answers might include: All the teenage characters develop. Alem goes from being dependent on his father, to fending for himself and refusing to give up his bike, and finally to becoming a respected peacemaker. Mustapha apologises to Alem, and then plays an important part in the campaign. Ruth learns to overcome her past experiences with Themba. Mrs Fitzgerald, however, still cannot talk about Themba. Even worse, Mr Kelo cannot accept his son's growing independence or consider that he could be wrong about the anti-deportation campaign. He fails to develop or adapt.

Pages 54–55
Quick Test
1. This is the only way he and Alem will legally be allowed to live and work in England.
2. He takes the cheese knife.
3. The soldiers represent the law in each country and yet they are violent and threatening towards the peaceful, law-abiding Kelo family.
4. He has great faith in it.
5. They do not have faith in the UK legal system. They think that a campaign is needed to put pressure on the system.

Exam Practice
Answers might include: The play clearly shows the adversarial nature of the UK's legal system. It seems fair in that lawyers are allowed to speak both for and against the view that the Kelos' lives will be at risk if they return to Ethiopia or Eritrea. However, it seems that the lawyer for the Secretary of State is ill informed in saying 'the risk to the lives of the appellants is minimal'. The play presents the adjudicator as compassionate but inflexible, offering 'condolences' for the death of Mrs Kelo, but saying a judgement cannot be 'based on emotions'.

Pages 58–59

Practice Questions

Use the mark scheme at the end of the Answers section to self-assess your strengths and weaknesses. The grade descriptors are included to help you assess your progress towards your target grade.

Pages 60–61

Quick Test

1. Understanding of the whole text, use of textual evidence, awareness of the relevance of context, a well-structured essay and accurate writing.
2. Planning focuses your thoughts and allows you to produce a well-structured essay.
3. There are eight marks available for using a range of accurate vocabulary, punctuation and spelling in order to convey your ideas clearly and effectively.

Exam Practice

Answers might explore: the ambiguity of Sweeney as a character – he is seemingly friendly at first, inviting Mustapha and Alem to play table tennis, but then simply demands Mustapha's chips, and gets them; the question of whether Sweeney genuinely believes Alem is insulting his family – which would make him seem over-sensitive (especially when he has just been saying that family 'messes you up') – or if he just wants an excuse to attack Alem; Sweeney's racist, anti-refugee attitude towards Alem, and its context, and how this changes when Sweeney sides with Alem against the bike mugger; Sweeney's motives in advising Alem against knife fights and stroking his face. Answers might analyse Mustapha's fear of Sweeney.

Pages 62–63

Exam Practice

Sample upgrade of paragraph 6: It is an unexpected development when Sweeney defends Alem against the bike mugger. He teases Alem about the cheese knife, playfully comparing him to a cheese-loving character in the comic film series *Wallace and Gromit*. This implies that Alem's cheese knife cannot be taken seriously as a weapon, and Alem cannot be taken seriously as a fighter. Sweeney strokes his face, which is an oddly tender gesture in the context of teenage boys trying to seem tough. He may find Alem attractive, or he could just be showing his power. It is also unexpected that Sweeney confides that his father 'Used to try and rearrange my face for me.' This explains why Sweeney is a bully, even suggesting that he thinks this has trapped him in a world of violence that Alem can still escape.

Pages 64–65

Exam Practice

Use the mark scheme at the end of the Answers section to self-assess your strengths and weaknesses. Work up from the bottom, putting a tick by things you have fully accomplished, a ½ by skills that are in place but need securing, and underlining areas that need particular development. The estimated grade boundaries are included so you can assess your progress towards your target grade.

Pages 66–67

Quick Test

1. Understanding of the whole text, use of textual evidence, awareness of the relevance of context, a well-structured essay and accurate writing.
2. Planning focuses your thoughts and allows you to produce a well-structured essay.
3. There are eight marks available for using a range of accurate vocabulary, punctuation and spelling in order to convey your ideas clearly and effectively.

Exam Practice

Answers might explore: the impact of the two flashback scenes, which show that there is no protection under the law in Ethiopia or Eritrea for the Kelos, a fact which could help to explain why Mr Kelo has such optimistic (even naïve) faith in the UK's legal system; the adversarial system in the UK: opposing lawyers for the Kelos and the Secretary of State have to argue their cases and attempt to persuade the judge; how Alem feels unprotected by the law, and therefore carries a knife, but also how he eventually finds a non-violent way to challenge the legal process in the anti-deportation campaign.

Pages 68–69

Exam Practice

Sample upgrade of paragraph 5: Zephaniah and Sissay show that conflict exists even in loving families. Mr Kelo, perhaps because of his Ethiopian cultural conditioning, and because he is out of touch with how Alem has had to grow up in England, cannot accept Alem arguing with him. Despite his love for Alem, he raises his hand to hit him, showing how challenged he must feel. The fact that he says 'Get out of my house!', when they are not even in his house, shows that in the heat of the moment he is falling back on a model of authoritarian parenting that is inappropriate in the situation. Even the loving Fitzgeralds have differences of opinion over Themba and Alem, but they never resort to physical violence.

Pages 70–71

Exam Practice

Use the mark scheme at the end of the Answers section to self-assess your strengths and weaknesses. Work up from the bottom, putting a tick by things you have fully accomplished, a ½ by skills that are in place but need securing, and underlining areas that need particular development. The estimated grade boundaries are included so you can assess your progress towards your target grade.

Grade	AO1 (16 marks)	AO3 (16 marks)	AO4 (8 marks)
6–7+	A convincing, well-structured essay that answers the question fully. Clear interpretation of a range of different aspects of the play. Quotations and references are well chosen and integrated into sentences. The response covers the whole play.	Exploration is linked to specific aspects of the play's contexts to show a detailed understanding. Context is integrated with interpretation.	Consistent high level of accuracy. Vocabulary and sentences are used to make ideas clear and precise.
4–5	A clear essay that always focuses on the exam question. Some interpretation of different aspects of the play. Quotations and references support ideas effectively. The response refers to different points in the play.	References to relevant aspects of context show a clear understanding.	Good level of accuracy. Vocabulary and sentences help to keep ideas clear.
2–3	The essay has some good ideas that are mostly relevant. There is an attempt to interpret a few aspects of the play. Some quotations and references are used to support the ideas.	Some awareness of how ideas in the play link to its context.	Reasonable level of accuracy. Errors do not get in the way of the essay making sense.